The Writing on the Wall

and Other Literary

Essays

Other books by Mary McCarthy

Mary McCarthy

The Writing on the Wall and Other Literary Essays

Harcourt, Brace & World, Inc.　New York

Cui dono lepidum nouum libellum
Arido modo pumice expolitum?

To William Jovanovich
with love

Contents

The Writing on the Wall
and Other Literary
Essays

General Macbeth

HE is a general and has just won a battle; he enters the scene making a remark about the weather. "So foul and fair a day I have not seen." On this flat note Macbeth's character tone is set. "Terrible weather we're having." "The sun can't seem to make up its mind." "Is it hot/cold/wet enough for you?" A commonplace man who talks in commonplaces, a golfer, one might guess, on the Scottish fairways, Macbeth is the only Shakespeare hero who corresponds to a bourgeois type: a murderous Babbitt, let us say.

You might argue just the opposite, that Macbeth is over-imaginative, the prey of visions. It is true that he is impressionable. Banquo, when they come upon the witches, amuses himself at their expense, like a man of parts idly chaffing a fortune-teller. Macbeth, though, is deeply impressed. "Thane of Cawdor and King." He thinks this over aloud. "How can I be Thane of Cawdor when the Thane of Cawdor is alive?" When this mental stumbling-block has been cleared away for him (the Thane of Cawdor has received a death sentence), he turns his thoughts *sotto voce* to the next question. "How can I be King when Duncan is alive?" The answer comes back, "Kill him." It does fleetingly occur to Macbeth, as it would to most people, to leave matters alone and let destiny work it out. "If chance will have me King, why, chance may crown me, Without my stir." But this goes against his grain. A reflective man might wonder how fate would spin her plot, as

3

the Virgin Mary must have wondered after the Angel Gabriel's visit. But Macbeth does not trust to fate, that is, to the unknown, the mystery of things; he trusts only to a known quantity—himself—to put the prophecy into action. In short, he has no faith, which requires imagination. He is literal-minded; that, in a word, is his tragedy.

It was not *his* idea, he could plead in self-defense, but the witches', that he should have the throne. *They* said it first. But the witches only voiced a thought that was already in his mind; after all, he was Duncan's cousin and close to the crown. And once the thought has been put into *words,* he is in a scrambling hurry. He cannot wait to get home to tell his wife about the promise; in his excitement, he puts it in a letter, which he sends on ahead, like a businessman briefing an associate on a piece of good news for the firm.

Lady Macbeth takes very little stock in the witches. She never pesters her husband, as most wives would, with questions about the Weird Sisters: "What did they say, exactly?" "How did they look?" "Are you sure?" She is less interested in "fate and metaphysical aid" than in the business at hand—how to nerve her husband to do what he wants to do. And later, when Macbeth announces that he is going out to consult the Weird Sisters again, she refrains from comment. As though she were keeping her opinion—"O proper stuff!"—to herself. Lady Macbeth is not superstitious. Macbeth is. This makes her repeatedly impatient with him, for Macbeth, like many men of his sort, is an old story to his wife. A tale full of sound and fury signifying nothing. Her contempt for him perhaps extends even to his ambition. "Wouldst not play false, And yet wouldst wrongly win." As though to say, "All right, if that's what you want, have the courage to get it." Lady Macbeth does not so much give the impression of coveting the crown herself as of being weary of watching Macbeth covet it. Macbeth, by the way, is her second husband, and either her first husband was a better man than he, which galls her, or he was just another general, another superstitious golfer, which would gall her too.

Superstition here is the opposite of reason on the one hand and of imagination on the other. Macbeth is credulous, in contrast to Lady Macbeth, to Banquo, and, later, to Malcolm, who sets the audience an example of the right way by mistrusting Macduff until he has submitted him to an empirical test. Believing and knowing are paired in Malcolm's mind; what he *knows* he believes. Macbeth's eagerness to believe is the companion of his lack of faith. If all works out right for him in this world, Macbeth says, he can take a chance on the next ("We'd jump the life to come"). Superstition whispers when true religion has been silenced, and Macbeth becomes a ready client for the patent medicines brewed by the jeering witches on the heath.

As in his first interview with them he is too quick to act literally on a dark saying, in the second he is too easily reassured. He will not be conquered till "great Birnam Wood to high Dunsinane Hill shall come against him." "Why, that can never happen!" he cries out in immediate relief, his brow clearing.

It never enters his mind to examine the saying more closely, test it, so to speak, for a double bottom, as was common in those days (Banquo even points this out to him) with prophetic utterances, which were known to be ambiguous and tricky. Any child knew that a prophecy often meant the reverse of what it seemed to say, and any man of imagination would ask himself how Birnam Wood *might* come to Dunsinane and take measures to prevent it, as King Laius took measures to prevent his own death by arranging to have the baby Oedipus killed. If Macbeth had thought it out, he could have had Birnam Wood chopped down and burned on the spot and the ashes dumped into the sea. True, the prophecy might still have turned against him (since destiny cannot be avoided and the appointment will be kept at Samarra), but that would have been another story, another tragedy, the tragedy of a clever man not clever enough to circumvent fate. Macbeth is not clever; he is taken in by surfaces, by appearance. He cannot think beyond the usual course of things. "None of woman born." All men, he says to himself, sagely, are born of women; Malcolm and Macduff are men; therefore I am safe. This logic leaves out of account the extraordinary: the man brought into the world by Caesarean section. In the same way, it leaves out of account the supernatural—the very forces he is trafficking with. He might be overcome by an angel or a demon, as well as by Macduff.

Yet this pedestrian general sees ghosts and imaginary daggers in the air. Lady Macbeth does not, and the tendency in her husband grates on her nerves; she is sick of his terrors and fancies. A practical woman, Lady Macbeth, more a partner than a wife, though Macbeth treats her with a trite domestic fondness—"Love," "Dearest love," "Dearest chuck," "Sweet remembrancer." These middle-aged, middle-class endearments, as though he called her "Honeybunch" or "Sweetheart," as well as the obligatory "Dear," are a master stroke of Shakespeare's and perfectly in keeping with the prosing about the weather, the heavy credulousness.

Naturally Macbeth is dominated by his wife. He is old Iron Pants in the field (as she bitterly reminds him), but at home *she* has to wear the pants; she has to unsex herself. No "chucks" or "dearests" escape her tightened lips, and yet she is more feeling, more human finally than Macbeth. She thinks of her father when she sees the old King asleep, and this natural thought will not let her kill him. Macbeth has to do it, just as the quailing husband of any modern virago is sent down to the basement to kill a rat or drown a set of kittens. An image of her father, irrelevant to her purpose, softens this monster woman; sleepwalking, she thinks of Lady Macduff. "The Thane of Fife had a wife. Where is she now?" Stronger than Macbeth, less suggestible, she is nevertheless imaginative, where he is not. She does not see ghosts and daggers; when she sleepwalks, it is simple reality that haunts her—the crime relived. "Yet, who would have thought the old man to have had so much blood in him?" Over and over, the epiphenomena of the crime present themselves to her dormant consciousness. This nightly reliving is not penitence but more terrible—remorse, the agenbite of the restless deed. Lady Macbeth's uncontrollable imagination drives her to put herself in the place of others—the wife of the Thane of Fife—and to recognize a kinship between all human kind: the pathos of old age in Duncan has made her think, "Why, he might be my father!" This sense of a natural bond between men opens her to contrition—sorrowing with. To ask whether, waking, she is "sorry" for what she has done is impertinent. She lives with it and it kills her.

Macbeth has no feeling for others, except envy, a common middle-class trait. He *envies* the murdered Duncan his rest, which is a strange way of looking at your victim. What he suffers on his own account after the crimes is simple panic. He is never contrite or remorseful; it is not the deed but a shadow of it, Banquo's spook, that appears to him. The "scruples" that agitate him before Duncan's murder are mere echoes of conventional opinion, of what might be *said* about his deed: that Duncan was his king, his cousin, and a guest under his roof. "I have bought golden opinions," he says to himself (note the verb), "from all sorts of people"; now these people may ask for their opinions back—a refund—if they suspect him of the murder. It is like a business firm's being reluctant to part with its "good will." The fact that Duncan was such a good king bothers him, and why? Because there will be universal grief at his death. But his chief "scruple" is even simpler. "If we should fail?" he says timidly to Lady Macbeth. Sweet chuck tells him that they will not. Yet once she has ceased to be effectual as a partner, Dearest love is an embarrassment. He has no time for her vapors. "Cure her of that," he orders the doctor on hearing that she is troubled by "fancies." Again the general is speaking.

The idea of Macbeth as a conscience-tormented man is a platitude as false as Macbeth himself. Macbeth has no conscience. His main concern throughout the play is that most selfish of all concerns: to get a good night's sleep. His invocation to sleep, while heartfelt, is perfectly conventional; sleep builds you up, enables you to start the day fresh. Thus the virtue of having a good conscience is seen by him in terms of bodily hygiene. Lady Macbeth shares these preoccupations. When he tells her he is going to see the witches, she remarks that he needs sleep.

Her wifely concern is mechanical and far from real solicitude. She is aware of Macbeth; she *knows* him (he does not know her at all, apparently), but she regards him coldly as a thing, a tool that must be oiled and polished. His soul-states do not interest her; her attention is narrowed on his morale, his public conduct, the shifting expressions of his face. But in a sense she is right, for there is nothing to Macbeth but fear and ambition, both of which he tries to hide, except from her. This naturally gives her a poor opinion of the inner man.

Why is it, though, that Lady Macbeth seems to us a monster while Macbeth does not? Partly because she is a woman and has "unsexed" herself, which makes her a monster by definition. Also because the very prospect of murder quickens an hysterical excitement in her, like the discovery of some object in a shop—a set of emeralds or a sable stole—which Macbeth can give her and which will be an "outlet" for all the repressed desires he cannot satisfy. She behaves as though Macbeth, through his weakness, will deprive her of self-realization; the unimpeded exercise of her will is the voluptuous end she seeks. That is why she makes naught of scruples, as inner brakes on her throbbing engines. Unlike Macbeth, she does not pretend to harbor a conscience, though this, on her part, by a curious turn, *is* a pretense, as the sleepwalking scene reveals. After the first crime, her will subsides, spent; the devil has brought her to climax and left her.

Macbeth is not a monster, like Richard III or Iago or Iachimo, though in the catalogue he might go for one because of the blackness of his deeds. But at the outset his deeds are only the wishes and fears of the average, undistinguished man translated into halfhearted action. Pure evil is a kind of transcendence that he does not aspire to. He only wants to be king and sleep the sleep of the just, undisturbed. He could never have been a good man, even if he had not met the witches; hence we cannot see him as a devil incarnate, for the devil is a fallen angel. Macbeth does not fall; if anything, he somewhat improves as the result of his career of crime. He throws off his dependency and thus achieves the "greatness" he mistakenly sought in the crown and scepter. He swells to vast proportions, having supped full with horrors.

The isolation of Macbeth, which is at once a punishment and a tragic dignity or honor, takes place by stages and by deliberate choice; it begins when he does not tell Lady Macbeth that he has decided to kill Banquo and reaches its peak at Dunsinane, in the final action. Up to this time, though he has cut himself off from all human contacts, he is counting on the witches as allies. When he first hears the news that Macduff is not "of woman born," he is unmanned; everything he trusted (the literal word) has betrayed him, and he screams in terror, "I'll not fight with thee!" But Macduff's taunts make a hero of him; he cannot die like this, shamed. His death is his first true act of courage, though even here he has had to be pricked to it by mockery, Lady Macbeth's old spur. Nevertheless, weaned by his very crimes from a need for reassurance, nursed in a tyrant's solitude, he meets death on his own, without metaphysical aid. "Lay on, Macduff."

What is modern and bourgeois in Macbeth's character is his wholly *social* outlook. He has no feeling for others, and yet until the end he is a vicarious creature, existing in his own eyes through what others may say of him, through what they tell him or promise him. This paradox is typical of the social being—at once a wolf out for himself and a sheep. Macbeth, moreover, is an expert buck-passer; he sees how others can be used. It is he, not Lady Macbeth, who thinks of smearing the drunken chamberlains with blood (though it is she, in the end, who carries it out), so that they shall be caught "red-handed" the next morning when Duncan's murder is discovered. At this idea he brightens; suddenly, he sees his way clear. It is the moment when at last he decides. The eternal executive, ready to fix responsibility on a subordinate, has seen the deed finally take a *recognizable* form. Now he can do it. And the crackerjack thought of killing the grooms afterward (dead men tell no tales—old adage) is again purely his own on-the-spot inspiration; no credit to Lady Macbeth.

It is the sort of thought that would have come to Hamlet's Uncle Claudius, another trepidant executive. Indeed, Macbeth is more like Claudius than like any other character in Shakespeare. Both are doting husbands; both rose to power by betraying their superior's trust; both are easily frightened and have difficulty saying their prayers. Macbeth's "Amen" sticks in his throat, he complains, and Claudius, on his knees, sighs that he cannot make what priests call a "good act of contrition." The desire to say his prayers like any pew-holder, quite regardless of his horrible crime, is merely a longing for respectability. Macbeth "repents" killing the grooms, but this is for public consumption. "O, yet I do repent me of my fury, That I did kill them." In fact, it is the one deed he does *not* repent (*i.e.,* doubt the wisdom of) either before or after. This hypocritical self-accusation, which is his sidelong way of announcing the embarrassing fact that he has just done away with the grooms, and his simulated grief at Duncan's murder ("All is but toys. Renown and grace is dead, The wine of life is drawn," etc.) are his basest moments in the play, as well as his boldest; here is nearly a magnificent monster.

The dramatic effect too is one of great boldness on Shakespeare's part. Macbeth is speaking pure Shakespearean poetry, but in his mouth, since we know he is lying, it turns into facile verse, Shakespearean poetry buskined. The same with "Here lay Duncan, His silver skin lac'd with his golden blood. . . ." If the image were given to Macduff, it would be uncontaminated poetry; from Macbeth it is "proper stuff"—fustian. This opens the perilous question of sincerity in the arts: is a line of verse altered for us by the sincerity of the one who speaks it? In short, is poetry relative to the circumstances or absolute? Or, more particularly, are Macbeth's soliloquies poetry, which they sound like, or something else? Did Shakespeare intend to make Macbeth a poet, like Hamlet, Lear, and Othello? In that case, how can Macbeth be an unimaginative mediocrity? My opinion is that Macbeth's soliloquies are not poetry but rhetoric. They are tirades. That is, they do not trace any pensive motion of the soul or heart but are a volley of words discharged. Macbeth is neither thinking nor feeling aloud; he is declaiming. Like so many unfeeling men, he has a facile emotionalism, which he turns on and off. Not that his fear is insincere, but his loss of control provides him with an excuse for histrionics.

These gibberings exasperate Lady Macbeth. "What do you mean?" she says coldly after she has listened to a short harangue on "Methought I heard a voice cry 'Sleep no more!' " It is an allowable question—what *does* he mean? And his funeral oration on *her,* if she could have heard it, would have brought her back to life to protest. "She should have died hereafter"—fine, that was the real Macbeth. But then, as if conscious of the proprieties, he at once begins on a series of bromides ("Tomorrow, and tomorrow . . .") that he seems to have had ready to hand for the occasion like a black mourning suit. All Macbeth's soliloquies have that ready-to-hand, if not hand-me-down, air, which is perhaps why they are given to school children to memorize, often with the result of making them hate Shakespeare. What children resent in these soliloquies is precisely their sententiousness—the sound they have of being already memorized from a copybook.

Macbeth's speeches often recall the Player's speech in *Hamlet*—Shakespeare's example of how-not-to-do-it. He tears a passion to tatters. He has a rather Senecan rhetoric, the fustian of the time; in the dagger speech, for example, he works in Hecate, Tarquin, and the wolf—recherché embellishment for a man who is about to commit a real murder. His taste for hyperbole goes with a habit of euphuism, as when he calls the sea "the green one." And what of the remarkable line just preceding, "The multitudinous seas incarnadine," with its onomatopoeia of the crested waves rising in the t's and d's of "multitudinous" and subsiding in the long swell of the verb? This is sometimes cited as an example of pure poetry, which it would be in an anthology of isolated lines, but in the context, dramatically, it is splendid bombast, a kind of stuffing or padding.

The play between poetry and rhetoric, the *conversion* of poetry to declamation, is subtle and horrible in *Macbeth*. The sincere pent-up poet in Macbeth flashes out not in the soliloquies but when he howls at a servant. "The Devil damn thee black, thou cream-faced loon! Where got'st thou that goose look?" Elsewhere, the general's tropes are the gold braid of his dress uniform or the chasing of his armor. If an explanation is needed, you might say he learned to *use* words through long practice in haranguing his troops, whipping them and himself into battle frenzy. Up to recent times a fighting general, like a football coach, was an orator.

But it must be noted that it is not only Macbeth who rants. Nor is it only Macbeth who talks about the weather. The play is stormy with atmosphere—the screaming and shrieking of owls, the howling of winds. Nature herself is ranting, like the witches, and Night, black Hecate, is queen of the scene. Bats are flitting about; ravens and crows are hoarse; the house-martins' nests on the battlements of Macbeth's castle give a misleading promise of peace and gentle domesticity. "It will be rain tonight," says Banquo simply, looking at the sky (note the difference between this and Macbeth's pompous generality), and the First Murderer growls at him, striking, "Let it come down." The disorder of Nature, as so often in Shakespeare, presages and reflects the disorder of the body politic. Guilty Macbeth cannot sleep, but the night of Duncan's murder, the whole house, as if guilty too, is restless; Malcolm and Donalbain talk and laugh in their sleep; the drunken porter, roused, plays that he is gatekeeper of hell.

Indeed, the whole action takes place in a kind of hell and is pitched to the demons' shriek of hyperbole. This would appear to be a peculiar setting for a study of the commonplace. But only at first sight. The fact that an ordinary philistine like Macbeth goes on the rampage and commits a series of murders is a sign that human nature, like Nature, is capable of any mischief if left to its "natural" self. The witches, unnatural beings, are Nature spirits, stirring their snake-filet and owl's wing, newt's eye and frog toe in a camp stew: earthy ingredients boil down to an unearthly broth. It is the same with the man Macbeth. Ordinary ambition, fear, and a kind of stupidity make a deadly combination. Macbeth, a self-made king, is not kingly, but just another Adam or Fall guy, with Eve at his elbow.

There is no play of Shakespeare's (I think) that contains the words "Nature" and "natural" so many times, and the "Nature" within the same speech can mean first something good and then something evil, as though it were a pun. Nature is two-sided, double-talking, like the witches. "Fair is foul and foul is fair," they cry, and Macbeth enters the play unconsciously echoing them, for he is never original but chock-full of the "milk of human kindness," which does not mean kindness in the modern sense but simply human "nature," human kind. The play is about Nature, and its blind echo, human nature.

Macbeth, in short, shows life in the cave. Without religion, animism rules the outer world, and without faith, the human soul is beset by hobgoblins. This at any rate was Shakespeare's opinion, to which modern history, with the return of the irrational in the Fascist nightmare and its fear of new specters in the form of Communism, Socialism, etc., lends support. It is a troubling thought that bloodstained Macbeth, of all Shakespeare's characters, should seem the most "modern," the only one you could transpose into contemporary battle dress or a sport shirt and slacks.

The contemporary Macbeth, a churchgoer, is indifferent to religion, to the categorical imperative or any group of principles that may be held to stand above and govern human behavior. Like the old Macbeth, he'd gladly hazard the future life, not only for himself but for the rest of humanity: "Though palaces and pyramids do slope Their heads to their foundations; though the treasure Of Nature's germens tumble all together . . ." He listens to soothsayers and prophets and has been out on the heath and in the desert, putting questions to Nature on a grand scale, lest his rivals for power get ahead of him and Banquo's stock, instead of his, inherit the earth. Unloosing the potential destructiveness that was always there in Nature, as Shakespeare understood, the contemporary Macbeth, like the old one, is not even a monster, though he may yet breed monsters, thanks to his activities on the heath; he is timorous, unimaginative, and the prayer he would like to say most fervently is simply "Amen."

June, 1962

A Bolt from the Blue

*P**ALE FIRE* is a Jack-in-the-box, a Fabergé gem, a clock-work toy, a chess problem, an infernal machine, a trap to catch reviewers, a cat-and-mouse game, a do-it-yourself kit. This new work by Vladimir Nabokov consists of a 999-line poem of four cantos in heroic couplets together with an editor's preface, notes, index, and proof corrections. When the separate parts are assembled, according to the manufacturer's directions, and fitted together with the help of clues and cross-references, which must be hunted down as in a paper-chase, a novel on several levels is revealed, and these "levels" are not the customary "levels of meaning" of modernist criticism but planes in a fictive space, rather like those houses of memory in medieval mnemonic science, where words, facts, and numbers were stored till wanted in various rooms and attics, or like the Houses of astrology into which the heavens are divided.

The poem has been written by a sixty-one-year-old American poet of the homely, deceptively homely, Robert Frost type who teaches at Wordsmith College in New Wye, Appalachia; his name is John Shade, his wife is called Sybil, née Irondell or Swallow; his parents were ornithologists; he and his wife had a fat, plain daughter, Hazel, who killed herself young by drowning in a lake near the campus. Shade's academic "field" is Pope, and his poem, *Pale Fire,* is in Pope's heroic measure; in content, it is closer to Wordsworthian pastures—rambling, autobiographical, full of childhood memories, gleanings from Nature, interrogations of the universe: a kind of American *Prelude*. The commentator is Shade's colleague, a refugee professor from Zembla, a mythical country north of Russia. His name is Charles Kinbote; he lives next door to Shade in a house he has rented from Judge Goldsworth, of the law faculty, absent on sabbatical leave. (If, as the commentator points out, you recombine the syllables of "Wordsmith" and "Goldsworth," you get Goldsmith and Wordsworth, two masters of the heroic couplet.) At the moment of writing, Kinbote has fled Appalachia and is living in a log cabin in a motor court at Cedarn in the Southwest; Shade has been murdered, fortuitously, by a killer calling himself Jack Grey, and Kinbote, with the widow's permission, has taken his manuscript to edit in hiding, far from the machinations of two rival Shadians on the faculty. Kinbote, known on the campus as the Great Beaver, is a bearded vegetarian pederast, who has had bad luck with his youthful "ping-pong partners"; a lonely philologue and long-standing admirer of the poet (he has translated him into Zemblan), he has the unfortunate habit of "dropping in" on the Shades, spying on them (they don't draw theirs) with binoculars from a post at a window or in the shrubbery; jealous of Mrs. Shade, he is always available for a game of chess or a "good ramble" with the tolerant poet, whom he tirelessly entertains with his Zemblan reminiscences. "I fail to see how John and Sybil can stand you," a faculty wife hisses at him in the grocery store. "What's more, you are insane."

That is the plot's ground floor. Then comes the *piano nobile*. Kinbote believes that he has inspired his friend with his tales of his native Zembla, of its exiled king, Charles the Beloved, and the Revolution that started in the Glass Works; indeed, he has convinced himself that the poem is *his* poem—the occupational mania of commentators—and cannot be properly understood without his gloss, which narrates Zemblan events paralleling the poet's composition. What at once irresistibly peeps out from Kinbote's notes is that he himself is none other than Charles the Beloved, disguised in a beaver as an academic; he escaped from Zembla in a motorboat and flew to America after a short stay on the Côte d'Azur; an American sympathizer, a trustee of Wordsmith, Mrs. Sylvia O'Donnell, has found him a post on the language faculty. His colleagues (read "mortal enemies") include—besides burly Professor Hurley, head of the department and an adherent of *"engazhay"* literature—Professor C., a literary Freudian and owner of an ultra-modern villa, a certain Professor Pnin, and an instructor, Mr. Gerald Emerald, a young man in a bow tie and green velvet jacket. Meanwhile the Shadows, the Secret Police of Zembla, have hired a gunman, Jakob Gradus, alias Jacques d'Argus, alias Jacques Degré, alias Jack Grey, to do away with the royal exile. Gradus' slow descent on Wordsmith synchronizes, move by move, with Shade's composition of *Pale Fire;* the thug, wearing a brown suit, a trilby, and carrying a Browning, alights on the campus the day the poem is finished. In the library he converges with Mr. Gerald Emerald, who obligingly gives him a lift to Professor Kinbote's house. There, firing at the king, he kills the poet; when the police take him, he masks his real purpose and identity by claiming to be a lunatic escaped from a local asylum.

This second story, the *piano nobile,* is the "real" story as it appears to Kinbote of the events leading to the poet's death. But the real, real story, the story underneath, has been transpiring gradually, by degrees, to the reader. Kinbote is mad. He is a harmless refugee pedant named Botkin who teaches in the Russian department and who fancies himself to be the exiled king of Zembla. This delusion, which he supposes to be his secret, is known to the poet, who pities him, and to the campus at large, which does not—the insensate woman in the grocery store was expressing the general opinion. The killer is just what he claims to be—Jack Grey, an escaped criminal lunatic, who has been sent to the State Asylum for the Insane by, precisely, Judge Goldsworth, Botkin's landlord. It is Judge Goldsworth that the madman intended to murder, not Botkin, alias Kinbote, alias Charles the Beloved; the slain poet was the victim of a case of double mistaken identity (his poem, too, is murdered by its editor, who mistakes it for something else). The clue to Gradus-Grey, moreover, was in Botkin's hands when, early in the narrative, he leafed through a sentimental album kept by the judge containing photographs of the killers he had sent to prison or condemned to death: ". . . a strangler's quite ordinary-looking hands, a self-made widow, the close-set merciless eyes of a homicidal maniac (somewhat resembling, I admit, the late Jacques d'Argus), a bright little parricide aged seven. . . ." He got, as it were, a preview of the coming film—a frequent occurrence in this kind of case. Projected onto Zembla, in fact, are the daily events of the campus. Gradus' boss, Uzumrudov, one of the higher Shadows, met on the Riviera in a green velvet jacket is slowly recognized to be "little Mr. Anon.," alias Gerald Emerald, alias Reginald Emerald, a teacher of freshman English, who has made advances to (read in reverse "had advances made to him by") Professor Botkin, and who is also the author of a rude anonymous note suggesting that Professor Botkin has halitosis. The paranoid political structure called Zembla in Botkin's exiled fantasy—with its Extremist government and secret agents—is a transliteration of a pederast's persecution complex, complicated by the "normal" conspiracy-mania of a faculty common room.

But there is in fact a "Zembla," behind the Iron Curtain. The real, real story, the plane of ordinary sanity and common sense, the reader's presumed plane, cannot be accepted as final. The explanation that Botkin is mad will totally satisfy only Professors H. and C. and their consorts, who can put aside *Pale Fire* as a detective story, with the reader racing the author to the solution. *Pale Fire* is not a detective story, though it includes one. Each plane or level in its shadow box proves to be a false bottom; there is an infinite perspective regression, for the book is a book of mirrors.

Shade's poem begins with a very beautiful image, of a bird that has flown against a window and smashed itself, mistaking the reflected sky in the glass for the true azure. "I was the shadow of the waxwing slain By the false azure in the windowpane." This image is followed by another, still more beautiful and poignant, a picture of that trick of optics whereby a room at night, when the shades have not been drawn, is reflected in the dark landscape outside.

> Uncurtaining the night, I'd let dark glass
> Hang all the furniture above the grass,
> And how delightful when a fall of snow
> Covered my glimpse of lawn and reached up so
> As to make chair and bed exactly stand
> Upon that snow, out in that crystal land!

"That crystal land," notes the commentator, loony Professor Botkin. "Perhaps an allusion to Zembla, my dear country." On the plane of everyday sanity, he errs. But on the plane of poetry and magic, he is speaking the simple truth, for Zembla is Semblance, Appearance, the mirror-realm, the Looking-Glass of Alice. This is the first clue in the treasure hunt, pointing the reader to the dual or punning nature of the whole work's composition. *Pale Fire,* a reflective poem, is also a prism of reflections. Zembla, the land of seeming, now governed by the Extremists, is the antipodes of Appalachia, in real homespun democratic America, but it is also the *semblable*, the twin, as seen in a distorting glass. Semblance becomes resemblance. John Shade and Gradus have the same birthday—July 5.

The word "Zembla" can be found in Pope's *Essay on Man* (Epistle 2, v); there it signifies the fabulous extreme north, the land of the polar star.

> But where the Extreme of Vice was ne'er agreed.
> Ask where's the North? At York, 'tis on the Tweed;
> In Scotland, at the Oroades, and there,
> At Greenland, Zembla, or the Lord knows where;
> No creature owns it in the first degree,
> But thinks his neighbor farther gone than he.

Pope is saying that vice, when you start to look for it, is always somewhere else—a will-o'-the-wisp. This somewhere else is Zembla, but it is also next door, at your neighbor's. Now Botkin is Shade's neighbor and vice versa; moreover, people who live in glass houses . . . Shade has a vice, the bottle, the festive glass, and Botkin's vice is that he is an *invert, i.e.,* turned upside down, as the antipodes are, relative to each other. Further, the reader will notice that the word "Extreme," with a capital (Zemblan Extremists), and the word "degree" (Gradus is degree in Russian) both occur in these verses of Pope, in the neighborhood of Zembla, pre-mirroring *Pale Fire,* as though by second sight. Reading on, you find (lines 267–268), the following couplet quoted by John Shade in a discarded variant of his own manuscript:

> See the blind beggar dance, the cripple sing,
> The sot a hero, lunatic a king . . .

The second line is *Pale Fire* in a nutshell. Pope continues (lines 269–270):

> The starving chemist in his golden views
> Supremely blest, the poet in his muse.

Supremely Blest is the title of John Shade's book on Pope. In this section of the poem, Pope is playing on the light-and-shade antithesis and on what an editor calls the "pattern of paradoxical attitudes" to which man's dual nature is subject. The lunatic Botkin incidentally, playing king, *inverts* his name.

To leave Pope momentarily and return to Zembla, there is an actual Nova Zembla, a group of islands in the Arctic

Ocean, north of Archangel. The name is derived from the Russian *Novaya Zemlya,* which means "new land." Or *Terre Neuve,* Newfoundland, the New World. Therefore Appalachia = Zembla. But since for Pope Zembla was roughly equal to Greenland, then Zembla must be a green land, an Arcadia. Arcady is a name often bestowed by Professor Botkin on New Wye, Appalachia, which also gets the epithet "green," and he quotes *"Et in Arcadia ego,"* for Death has come to Arcady in the shape of Gradus, ex-glazier and killer, the emissary of Zembla on the other side of the world. Green-jacketed Gerald Emerald gives Death a lift in his car.

The complementary color to green is red. Zembla has turned red after the Revolution that began in the Glass Factory. Green and red flash on and off in the narrative like traffic signals and sometimes reverse their message. Green appears to be the color of death, and red the color of life; red is the king's color and green the color of his enemies. Green is pre-eminently the color of seeming (the theatrical green-room), the color, too, of camouflage, for Nature, being green at least in summer, can hide a green-clad figure in her verdure. But red is a color that is dangerous to a wearer who is trying to melt into the surroundings. The king escapes from his royal prison wearing a red wool cap and sweater (donned in the dark) and he is only saved by the fact that forty loyal Karlists, his supporters, put on red wool caps and sweaters, too (red wool yarn—"yarn" comes from Latin "soothsayer" —is protective Russian folk magic) and confuse the Shadows with a multitude of false kings. Yet when the king arrives in America he floats down with a green silk parachute (because he is in disguise?), and his gardener at New Wye, a Negro whom he calls Balthasar (the black king of the three Magi), has a green thumb, a red sweater, and is seen on a green ladder; it is the gardener who saves the king's life when Gradus, alias Grey, appears.

Now when Alice went through the looking-glass she entered a chess game as a white pawn. There is surely a chess game or chess problem in *Pale Fire,* played on a board of green and red squares. The poet describes his residence as "the frame house between Goldsworth and Wordsmith on its square of green"; the Rose Court in the royal palace in Onhava (Far Away), the Zemblan capital, is a sectile mosaic with rose petals cut out of red stone and large thorns cut out of green marble. There is much stress, in place descriptions, on framing, and reference is made to chess problems of "the solus rex type." The royal fugitive may be likened to a lone king running away on the board. But in problems of the solus rex type, the king, though outnumbered, is, curiously enough, not always at a disadvantage; for example, a king and two knights cannot checkmate a lone king—the game is stalemated or drawn. All the chess games played by characters in the story are draws. The plot of the novel ends in a kind of draw, if not a stalemate. The king's escape from the castle is doubtless castling.

Chess is the perfect mirror-game, with the pieces drawn up confronting each other as in a looking-glass; moreover, castles, knights, and bishops have their twins as well as their opposite numbers. The piece, by the way, called the bishop in English in French is *"le fou"* or madman. In the book there are two opposed lunatics at large: Gradus and Kinbote. The moves made by Gradus from the Zemblan capital to Wordsmith in New Wye parallel spatially the moves made in time by the poet toward the completion of his poem; at the zero hour, there is a convergence of space and time. What is shadowed forth here may be a game of three-dimensional chess—three simultaneous games played by a pair of chess wizards on three transparent boards arranged vertically. A framed crystal land, the depth-echo of the bedroom projected onto the snow.

The moves of Gradus also hint some astrological progression. Botkin reached Judge Goldsworth's "chateau" on Feb-

ruary 5, 1959; on Monday, February 16, he was introduced
to the poet at lunch at the Faculty Club; on March 14, he
dined at the Shades', etc. The magnum opus of old John
Shade is begun July 1; under the sign of Cancer, he walks
sideways, like a crab. The poem is completed (except for the
last line) the day of Gradus' arrival, July 21, on the cusp
between Cancer and Leo. As the poet walks to his death, the
sound of horseshoes is heard from a neighboring yard
(horseshoe crabs?). The fateful conjunction of three planets
seems to be indicated, and the old astrological notion of
events on earth mirroring the movements of the stars in the
sky.

The twinning and doubling proliferate; the multiplication of
levels casts a prismatic, opaline light on Faculty Row. Zembla is not just land but earth—"Terra the Fair, an orbicle of
jasp," as John Shade names the globe; a Zemblan feuilletonist
had fancifully dubbed its capital Uranograd—"Sky City."
The fate of Charles the Beloved is a rippling reflection of the
fate of Charles II of England on his travels, of Bonnie Prince
Charlie and of the deposed Shakespearean rulers for whom
streets are named in Onhava—Coriolanus Lane, Timon
Alley. Prospero of *The Tempest* pops in and out of the commentary, like a Fata Morgana, to mislead the reader into
looking for "pale fire" in Shakespeare's swan song. It is not
there, but *The Tempest* is in *Pale Fire:* Prospero's emerald
isle, called the Ile of Divels, in the New World, Iris, and
Juno's peacock, sea caves, the chess game of Ferdinand and
Miranda, Prospero's enchantments, his lost kingdom, and
Caliban, whom he taught language, that supreme miracle of
mirroring.

Nature's imitations of Nature are also evoked—echo, the
mocking-bird perched on a television aerial ("TV's huge pa-
perclip"), the iridescent eyes of the peacock's fan, the cica-
da's emerald case, a poplar tree's rabbit-foot—all the "natural shams" of protective mimicry by which, as Shade says in

his poem, "The reed becomes a bird, the knobby twig An inchworm, and the cobra head, a big Wickedly folded moth." These disguises are not different from the exiled king's red cap and sweater (like the markings of a bird) or the impersonation of an actor. Not only Nature's shams but Nature's freaks dance in and out of the lines: rings around the moon, rainbows and sun dogs (bright spots of light, often colored, sometimes seen on the ring of the solar halo), the heliotrope or sun-turner, which, by a trick of language, is also the bloodstone, Muscovy glass (mica), phosphorescence (named for Venus, the Morning Star), mirages, the roundlet of pale light called the *ignis fatuus,* fireflies, everything speckled, freckled, curiously patterned, dappled, quaint (as in Hopkins' poem "Pied Beauty"). The arrowy tracks of the pheasant, the red heraldic barrings of the Vanessa butterfly, snow crystals. And the imitation of natural effects in manufactures: stained glass, paperweights containing snowstorms and mountain views, glass eyes. Not to mention curios like the bull's-eye lantern, glass giraffes, Cartesian devils. Botkin, the bearded urning, is himself a prime "freak of Nature," like Humbert Humbert. And freakish puns of language ("Red Sox Beat Yanks 5/4 on Chapman's Homer"), "muscat" (a cat-and-mouse game), anagrams, mirror-writing, such words as "versipel." The author loves the ampersand and dainty diminutives ending in "let" or "et" (nymphet). Rugged John Shade is addicted to "word-golf," which he induces Botkin to play with him. Botkin's best scores are hate-love in three (late-lave-love), lass-male in four (last-mast-malt-male), live-dead in five. If you play word-golf with the title words, you can get pale-hate in two and fire-love in three. Or pale-love in three and fire-hate in three.

The misunderstandings of scholarship, cases of mistaken word-identity, also enchant this dear author. *E.g.,* "alder-wood" and "alderking" keep cropping up in the gloss with overtones of northern forest magic. What can an alderking be, excluding chief or ruler, which would give king-king, a redundancy? *Erle* is the German word for alder, and the alder tree, which grows in wet places, has the curious property of not rotting under water. Hence it is a kind of magic tree, very useful for piles supporting bridges. And John Shade, writing of the loss of his daughter, echoes Goethe's "The Erl-King."

> Who rides so late in the night and the wind?
> It is the writer's grief. It is the wild
> March wind. It is the father with his child.

Now the German scholar Herder, in translating the elf-king story from the Danish, mistook the word for elf (*elle*) for the word for alder. So it is not really the alderking but the elf- or goblin-king, but the word "alder" touched by the enchanted word "elf" becomes enchanted itself and dangerous. Goethe's erl-king, notes Kinbote, fell in love with the traveler's little boy. Therefore alderking means an eerie, dangerous invert found in northern forest-countries. Similar sorcerers' tricks are played with the word "stone." The king in his red cap escaping through the Zemblan mountains is compared to a *Steinmann,* which, as Kinbote explains, is a pile of stones erected by alpinists to commemorate an ascent; these stone men, apparently, like snowmen, were finished off with a red cap and scarf. The *Steinmann,* then, becomes a synonym for one of the king's disguised followers in red cap and sweater (*e.g.,* Julius Steinmann, Zemblan patriot). But the *Steinmann* has another meaning, not divulged by Kinbote; it is the *homme de pierre* or *homme de St. Pierre* of Pushkin's poem about Don Giovanni, in short the stone statue, the Commendatore of the opera. Anyone who sups with the stone man, St. Peter's deputy, will be carried off to hell. The mountain that the *Steinmann*-king has to cross is wooded by Mandevil Forest; toward the end of his journey he meets a disguised figure, Baron Mandevil, man of fashion, catamite, and

Zemblan patriot. Read man-devil, but read also Sir John Mandeville, medieval impostor and author of a book of voyages who posed as an English knight (perhaps a chess move is indicated?). Finally the stone (glancing by glass houses) is simply the stone thrown into a pool or lake and starting the tremulous magic of widening ripples that distort the clear mirroring of the image—as the word "stone" itself, cast into the pool of this paragraph has sent out wavelets in a widening circle.

Lakes—the original mirrors of primeval man—play an important part in the story. There are three lakes near the campus, Omega, Ozero, and Zero (Indian names, notes Botkin, garbled by early settlers); the king sees his consort, Disa, Duchess of Payn (sadism; theirs was a "white" marriage) mirrored in an Italian lake. The poet's daughter has drowned herself in Lake Omega; her name (". . . in lone Glenartney's hazel shade") is taken from *The Lady of the Lake*. But a hazel wand is also a divining-rod, used to find water; in her girlhood, the poor child, witch Hazel, was a poltergeist.

Trees, lakes, butterflies, stones, peacocks—there is also the waxwing, the poet's alter ego, which appears in the first line of the poem (duplicated in the last, unwritten line). If you look up the waxwing in the OED, you will find that it is "a passerine bird of the genus Ampelis, esp. A. garrulus, the Bohemian waxwing. Detached from the chatterers by Monsieur Vieillot." The poet, a Bohemian, is detached from the chatterers with whom he is easily confused. The waxwing (belonging to the king's party) has red-tipped quills like sealing wax. Another kind of waxwing is the Cedar Waxwing. Botkin has fled to Cedarn. The anagram of "Cedarn" is nacred.

More suggestively (in the popular sense), the anal canal or "back door" or *"porte étroite"* is linked with a secret passage leading by green-carpeted stairs to a green door (which in turn leads to the greenroom of the Onhava National Theatre), discovered by the king and a boyhood bedfellow. It is through this secret passage (made for Iris Acht, a leading actress) that the king makes his escape from the castle. Elsewhere a "throne," in the child's sense of "the toilet," is identified naughtily with the king. When gluttonous Gradus arrives in Appalachia, he is suffering from a severe case of diarrhea, induced by a conflict of "French" fries, consumed in a Broadway restaurant, with a genuine French ham sandwich, which he had saved from his Nice-Paris railway trip. The discharge of his bowels is horribly paralleled with the discharge of the automatic pistol he is carrying; he is the modern automatic man. In discharging the chamber of his pistol he is exercising what to him is a "natural" function; earlier the slight sensory pleasure he will derive from the act of murder is compared to the pleasure a man gets from squeezing a blackhead.

This is no giggling, high-pitched, literary camp. The repetitions, reflections, misprints, and quirks of Nature are the stamp or watermark of a god or supreme intelligence. There is a web of sense in creation, old John Shade decides—not text but texture, the warp and woof of coincidence. He hopes to find "some kind Of correlated pattern in the game, Plexed artistry, and something of the same Pleasure in it as they who played it found." The world is a sportive work of art, a mosaic, an iridescent tissue. Appearance and "reality" are interchangeable; all appearance, however deceptive, is real. Indeed it is just this faculty of deceptiveness (natural mimicry, trompe l'oeil, imposture), this power of imitation, that provides the key to Nature's cipher. Nature has "the artistic temperament"; the galaxies, if scanned, will be an iambic line.

Kinbote and Shade (and the author) agree in a detestation of symbols, except those of typography and, no doubt, natural science ("H_2O is a symbol for water"). They are believers in signs, pointers, blazes, notches, all of which point into a forest of associations, a forest in which other woodmen have left half-obliterated traces. All genuine works contain precognitions of other works or reminiscences of them (and in curved time the two are the same), just as the flying lizard already possessed a parachute, a fold of skin enabling it to glide through the air.

Shade, as an American, is an agnostic, and Kinbote, a European, is a vague sort of Christian who speaks of accepting "God's presence—a faint phosphorescence at first, a pale light in the dimness of bodily life, and a dazzling radiance after it." Or, more concessive, "Somehow Mind is involved as a main factor in the making of the universe." This Mind of Kinbote's seems to express itself most lucidly in dualities, pairs, twins, puns, couplets, like the plots of Shakespeare's early comedies. But this is only to be expected if one recalls that to make a cutout heart or lacy design for Valentine's Day all a child needs is a scissors and a folded piece of paper—the fold makes the pattern, which, unfolded, appears as a miracle. It is the quaint principle of the butterfly. Similarly, Renaissance artificers used to make wondrous "natural" patterns by bisecting a veined stone, an agate or a carnelian, as you would bisect an orange. Another kind of magic is the child's trick of putting a piece of paper on the cover of a schoolbook and shading it with a pencil; wonderfully, the stamped title, *Caesar's Gallic Wars,* emerges, as though embossed, in white letters. This, upside down, is the principle of the pheasant's hieroglyph in the snow or the ripple marks on the sand, to which we cry "How beautiful!" There is no doubt that duplication, stamping, printing (children's transfers), is one of the chief forms of magic, a magic we also see in Jack Frost's writing on the window, in jet trails in the sky—an intelligent spirit seems to have signed them. But it is not only in symmetry and reproduction that the magic signature of Mind is discerned, but in the very imperfections of Nature's work, which appear as guarantees of authentic, hand-knit manufacture. That is, in those blemishes and freckles and streakings and moles already mentioned that are the sports of creation, and what is a vice but a mole?

Nabokov's tenderness for human eccentricity, for the freak, the "deviate," is partly the naturalist's taste for the curious. But his fond, wry compassion for the lone black piece on the board goes deeper than classificatory science or the collector's chop-licking. Love is the burden of *Pale Fire,* love and loss. Love is felt as a kind of homesickness, that yearning for union described by Plato, the pining for the other half of a once-whole body, the straining of the soul's black horse to unite with the white. The sense of loss in love, of separation (the room *beyond,* projected onto the snow, the phantom moves of the chess knight, that deviate piece, *off* the board's edge onto ghostly squares), binds mortal men in a common pattern—the elderly couple watching TV in a lighted room, and the "queer" neighbor watching *them* from his window. But it is most poignant in the outsider: the homely daughter stood up by her date, the refugee, the "queen," the bird smashed on the windowpane.

Pity is the password, says Shade, in a philosophical discussion with Kinbote; for the agnostic poet, there are only two sins, murder and the deliberate infliction of pain. In the exuberant high spirits, the wild laughter of the book, there is a cry of pure pain. The compassion of Nabokov stops violently short of Gradus, that grey, degraded being, the shadow of a Shade. The modern, mass-produced, jet-propelled, newspaper-digesting killer is described with a fury of intimate hatred; he is Death on the prowl. Unnatural Death is the natural enemy of the delicate, gauzy ephemerids who are Nabokov's special love. Kinbote makes an "anti-Darwinian" aphorism: "The one who kills is *always* his victim's inferior."

Gradus in his broad-brimmed hat, with his umbrella and black traveling bag, figures as a kind of Batman out of children's comic books, whirring darkly through space; yet he is also Mercury (the mercury stands at so many *degrees* in the thermometer; there is a headless statue of Mercury in the secret passage leading from the palace to the theatre), conductor of souls to the underworld, Zeus's undercover agent, god of commerce, travel, manual skill, and thievery. In short, a "Jack of small trades and a killer," as Kinbote calls Jacques d'Argus, who was a pharmacology student at one time (the caduceus) and a messenger boy for a firm of cardboard-box manufacturers; Mercury or Hermes was the slayer of the giant Argus put to watch on Io by Juno-Hera; the hundred eyes of Argus were set in the tail of the peacock, Juno's familiar. Hermes, born and worshipped in Arcady, is simply a stone or herm; he is thought to have been in early times the *daimon* that haunted a heap of stones (the *Steinmann* or grave-ghost), also the place-spirit of a roadside marker or milestone; as a road god, he was the obvious patron of traders and robbers. He was often represented as a rudimentary stock or stone with a human head carved on top and a phallus halfway up. The beheaded Gradus-d'Argus has reverted to a rudimentary state of insentient stoniness—a sex-hater, he once tried to castrate himself.

Not only Hermes-Mercury, most of the nymphs of Arcady and gods of Olympus are glimpsed in *Pale Fire,* transformed, metamorphosed into animal or human shapes. Botkin is identified by Sybil Shade with the botfly, a kind of parasitic horsefly that infests sheep and cattle. Io, in cow form, was tormented by a gadfly sent by Hera; one of the Vanessa butterflies is the Io, marked with peacock eyes. Another is the Limenitis Sibylla, the White Admiral, and the Red Admiral is the Vanessa Atalanta, which feeds on wounded tree stems, like the scarred hickory in Shade's bosky garden. Atalanta was another Arcadian. The sibyls, on the other hand, are connected with Apollo, and Shade with his laurel trees is an Apollonian figure. But Sibyl was born Swallow; the land of Arcady was drained by swallow-holes, and the first sibyl was daughter of Dardanus, ancestor of the Trojans, an Arcadian king. The Hyperboreans (read Zemblans) were a legendary people sacred to Apollo living behind the north wind in a land of perpetual sunshine—a counter-Arcadia. Zeus, the sky-king, is heard in the thunderstorms that occur at crucial moments in the Zemblan story—at the arrival of Gradus in America and in Mandevil Forest, on Mount Mandevil, when the king is making his escape; Zeus's thunderbolts, in classical times, were stones too, by which oaths were sworn.

The Arcadians and Olympians of *Pale Fire* are meteoric fugitives, like the deposed Kinbote, fitfully apprehended in a name, a passing allusion. Shade's ornithologist mother was called Caroline Lukin—a triple reference to the Carolina waxwing, to Apollo Lukeios, and to the sacred wood, *lucus,* in Latin, full of singing birds? A reference to the Pléiade edition of Proust conjures up the Pleiades, daughters of Atlas, who were turned into stars and set in the constellation Taurus. One of the seven Pleiades is Electra, "the shining one"; the word "electricity" in Greek was the word for amber, which was sent to Delphian Apollo by his Hyperboreans in the north. Shade has written a poem about electricity. But the Pleiad was also a group of seven poets who sought to revive tragedy at the court of Ptolemy Philadelphus in Alexandria, one of whom, Lykophron, was the author of a curious riddling poem, like *Pale Fire* one of the hermetic puzzles of its time, called the *Alexandra*—another name for Cassandra, Priam's daughter, who was loved by Apollo.

Amid such myriads of mica-like references to gods, nymphs, and demons there is hardly a glance at Christian myth and legend. I have found only two: the oblique allusion to St. Peter as gatekeeper of Heaven and the chess-jesting one to the Black King of the Magi. The book is adamantly classical, magical, and scientific. The author's attitude toward the mystery of the universe is nearer to the old herborist's charmed wonder than to the modern physicist's "faith." His practical morality is not far from Kant's, while his practical pantheism contains Platonic gleams: Kinbote's "phosphorescence" recalls the cave myth. Kinbote reverts to this notion when he concedes in his final remarks that Shade's *Pale Fire,* for all its deficiencies, has "echoes and wavelets of fire and pale phosphorescent hints" of the real Zemblan magic. This madman's concession may also be taken as the author's apology for his own work, in relation to the fiery Beyond of the pure imagination—the sphere of pure light or fire. But Plato's Empyrean is finished, a celestial storehouse or vault of models from which the forms of earthly life are copied. In Nabokov's view (see Shade's couplet, *"Man's life as commentary to abstruse Unfinished poem.* Note for future use"), the celestial Poem itself is incomplete.

The source of "pale fire" is *Timon of Athens,* Act IV, Scene 3, Timon speaking to the thieves:

> *". . . I'll example you with thievery:*
> *The sun's a thief, and with his great attraction*
> *Robs the vast sea; the moon's an arrant thief,*
> *And her pale fire she snatches from the sun;*
> *The sea's a thief . . ."*

This idea of natural thievery is bound up with the mirror-theme, for a mirror is held by primitive people to "steal" the image of the man it reflects, and all reflection, including poetic mimesis, can be regarded as a theft from reality, which in turn is always stealing ideas and plagiarizing from itself. It is only appropriate that thieving Mercury, patron of letters, "that transcendental tramp," as Kinbote calls Gradus, should be one of the work's principal characters. Botkin, in effect, has stolen Shade's poem. The moon, shining with her borrowed rays, appears in the Luna moth; Io, the cow, was originally a moon goddess, as is shown by her crescent horns. Shade's Aunt Maud had a verse book kept open at the index ("Moon, Moonrise, Moor, Moral"), and Shade's Webster is open at *M.* The sky-god Zeus's love affairs with various moon goddesses—*e.g.,* Europa as well as Io—are hinted at. Finally, the Red Admiral Vanessa butterfly, which accompanies the poet Shade like a herald of death into Botkin's garden, is often seen, as on that fatal day, at sunset; it has the unusual habit of flying at night, looking for its home—commonly a hollow tree; in other words, the Red Admiral is a butterfly that acts like its nocturnal double, a moth.

Pale Fire itself circles like a moth, or a moon, around Shakespeare's mighty flame. Hiding in the lines, there are many allusions to Shakespeare's plays, to his biography, to the trees mentioned in Shakespeare, and the treacherous color green may betray the presence of Shakespeare's enemy, the poet Robert Greene, who described the Bard as an upstart crow dressed in others' feathers; the crow, of course, is a thief. It is also the southernmost constellation, at the other pole from Zembla.

The pale fire of the title spreads beyond its original Shakespearean source and beacons toward a number of odd corners. In the commentary there is an account of the poet burning his rejected drafts in "the pale fire of the incinerator." An amusing sidelight is provided by the word "ingle," used by Kinbote to mean a catamite or boy favorite, but which also means blaze, from the Gaelic word for fire. I think too of the pale fire of opals and of Shelley, whose "incandescent soul" is mentioned in Shade's poem:

> Life like a dome of many-colored glass
> Stains the white radiance of eternity.

Whether the visible world, for Nabokov, is a prismatic reflection of eternity or the other way around is a central question that begs itself but that remains, for that very reason, moot and troubling. In the game of signaling back and forth with mirrors, which may be man's relation with the cosmos, there is perhaps no before or after, first or second, only distance—separation, exile—and across it, the agitated flashing of the semaphore.

In any case, this centaur-work of Nabokov's, half-poem,

half-prose, this merman of the deep, is a creature of perfect beauty, symmetry, strangeness, originality, and moral truth. Pretending to be a curio, it cannot disguise the fact that it is one of the very great works of art of this century, the modern novel that everyone thought was dead and that was only playing possum.

June, 1962

J. D. Salinger's Closed Circuit

WHO is to inherit the mantle of Papa Hemingway? Who if not J. D. Salinger? Holden Caulfield in *The Catcher in the Rye* has a brother in Hollywood who thinks *A Farewell to Arms* is terrific. Holden does not see how his brother, who is *his* favorite writer, can like a phony book like that. But the very image of the hero as pitiless phony-detector comes from Hemingway. In *Across the River and into the Trees,* the colonel gets a message on his private radar that a pock-marked writer he darkly spies across the room at Harry's Bar in Venice has "outlived his talents"—apparently some sort of crime. "I think he has the same pits on his heart and in his soul," confides the heroine, in her careful foreign English. That was Sinclair Lewis.

Like Hemingway, Salinger sees the world in terms of allies and enemies. He has a good deal of natural style, a cruel ear, a dislike of ideas (the enemy's intelligence system), and a ventriloquist's knack of disguising his voice. The artless dialect written by Holden is an artful ventriloquial trick of Salinger's, like the deliberate, halting English of Hemingway's waiters, fishermen, and peasants—anyone who speaks it is a good guy, a friend of the author's, to be trusted.

The Catcher in the Rye, like Hemingway's books, is based on a scheme of exclusiveness. The characters are divided into those who belong to the club and those who don't—the clean marlin, on the one hand, and the scavenger sharks on the other. Those who don't belong are "born that way"—headmasters, philanthropists, roommates, teachers of history and English, football coaches, girls who like the Lunts. They cannot help the way they are, the way they talk: they are obeying a law of species—even the pimping elevator operator, the greedy prostitute, the bisexual teacher of English who makes an approach to Holden in the dark.

It is not anybody's fault if just about everybody is excluded from the club in the long run—everybody but Ring Lardner, Thomas Hardy, Gatsby, Isak Dinesen, and Holden's little sister, Phoebe. In fact it is a pretty sad situation, and there is a real adolescent sadness and lonely desperation in *The Catcher in the Rye;* the passages where Holden, drunk and wild with grief, wanders like an errant pinball through New York at night are very good.

But did Salinger sympathize with Holden or vice versa? Stephen Dedalus in a similar situation met Mr. Bloom, but the only "good" person Holden meets is his little sister—himself in miniature or in glory, riding a big brown horse on a carousel and reaching for the gold ring. There is something false and sentimental here. Holden is supposed to be an outsider in his school, in the middle-class world, but he is really an insider with the track all to himself.

And now, ten years after *The Catcher in the Rye* we have *Franny and Zooey*. The book has been a best seller since *before* publication.

Again the theme is the good people against the stupid phonies, and the good is still all in the family, like the shares in a family-owned "closed" corporation. The heroes are or were seven children (two are dead), the wonderful Glass kids of a radio quiz show called "It's a Wise Child," half-Jewish, half-Irish, whose parents were a team of vaudevillians. These prodigies, nationally known and the subjects of many psychological studies, are now grown up: one is a writer-in-residence in a girls' junior college; one is a Jesuit priest; one is a housewife; one is a television actor (Zooey); and one is a student (Franny). They are all geniuses, but the greatest genius of them all was Seymour, who committed suicide on vacation in an early story of Salinger's called "A Perfect Day for Bananafish." Unlike the average genius, the Glass kids are good guys; they love each other and their parents and their cat and their goldfish, and they are expert phony-detectors. The dead sage Seymour has initiated them into Zen and other mystical cults.

During the course of the story, Franny has a little nervous breakdown, brought on by reading a small green religious book titled *The Way of a Pilgrim,* relating the quest for prayer of a simple Russian peasant. She is cured by her brother Zooey in two short séances between his professional television appointments; he recognizes the book (it was in Seymour's library, of course) and, on his own inspiration, without help from their older brother Buddy or from the Jesuit, teaches her that Jesus, whom she has been sweating to find via the Jesus Prayer, is not some fishy guru but just the Fat Lady in the audience, plain ordinary humanity with varicose veins, the you and me the performer has to reach if the show is going to click.

This democratic commercial is "sincere" in the style of an advertising man's necktie. The Jesus Zooey sells his sister is the old Bruce Barton Jesus—the word made flesh, Madison Avenue style. The Fat Lady is not quite everybody, despite Zooey's fast sales patter. She is the kind of everybody the wonderful Glass kids tolerantly accept. Jesus may be a television sponsor or a housewife or a television playwright or your Mother and Dad, but He (he?) cannot be an intellectual like Franny's horrible boy friend, Lane, who has written a paper on Flaubert and talks about Flaubert's "testicularity," or like his friend Wally, who, as Franny says plaintively, "looks like somebody who spent the summer in Italy or someplace."

These fakes and phonies are the outsiders who ruin everything. Zooey feels the same way. "I hate any kind of so-called creative type who gets on any kind of ship. I don't give a goddam what his reasons are." Zooey likes it here. He likes people, as he says, who wear horrible neckties and funny, padded suits, but he does not mind a man who dresses well and owns a two-cabin cruiser so long as he belongs to the real, native, video-viewing America. The wonderful Glass family has three radios, four portable phonographs, and a TV in their wonderful living room, and their wonderful, awesome medicine cabinet in the bathroom is full of sponsored products all of which have been loved by someone in the family.

The world of insiders, it would appear, has grown infinitely larger and more accommodating as Salinger has "matured." Where Holden Caulfield's club excluded just about everybody but his kid sister, Zooey's and Franny's secret society includes just about everybody but creative types and students and professors. Here exception is made, obviously, for the Glass family: Seymour, the poet and thinker, Buddy, the writer, and so on. They all have college degrees; the family bookshelves indicate a wide, democratic culture:

Dracula now stood next to *Elementary Pali, The Boy Allies at the Somme* stood next to *Bolts of Melody, The Scarab Murder Case* and *The Idiot* were together, *Nancy Drew and the Hidden Staircase* lay on top of *Fear and Trembling.*

The Glass family librarian does not discriminate, in keeping with the times, and books are encouraged to "mix." In Seymour's old bedroom, however, which is kept as a sort of temple to his memory, quotations, hand-lettered, from a select group of authors are displayed on the door: Marcus Aurelius, Issa, Tolstoy, Ring Lardner, Kafka, St. Francis de Sales, Mu Mon Kwan, etc. This honor roll is extremely institutional.

The broadening of the admissions policy—which is the text of Zooey's sermon—is more a propaganda aim, though, than an accomplishment. No doubt the author and his mouthpiece (who is smoking a panatela) would like to spread a message of charity. "Indiscrimination," as Seymour says in another Salinger story, ". . . leads to health and a kind of very real, enviable happiness." But this remark itself exhales an ineffable breath of gentle superiority. The club, for all its pep talks, remains a closed corporation, since the function of the Fat Lady, when you come down to it, is to be what?—an audience for the Glass kids, while the function of the Great Teachers is to act as their coaches and prompters. And who are these wonder kids but Salinger himself, splitting and multiplying like the original amoeba?

In Hemingway's work there was hardly anybody but Hemingway in a series of disguises, but at least there was only one Papa per book. To be confronted with the seven faces of Salinger, all wise and lovable and simple, is to gaze into a terrifying narcissus pool. Salinger's world contains nothing but Salinger, his teachers, and his tolerantly cherished audience—humanity. Outside are the phonies vainly signaling to be let in. They do not have the key, unlike the kids' Irish mother, Bessie, a home version of the Fat Lady, who keeps invading the bathroom while her handsome son Zooey is in the tub or shaving.

Sixty-eight pages of "Zooey" are laid in the family bathroom, the "throne" room, the holy-of-holies, the temple of the cult of self-worship. What methodical attention Salinger pays to Zooey's routines of shaving and bathing and nail-cleaning, as though these were priestly rituals performed by a god on himself. A numinous vapor, an *aura,* surrounds the mother, seated on the toilet, smoking and soliloquizing, while her son behind the figured shower curtain reads, smokes, bathes, answers. We have the sense of being present at a mystery: ablution, purification, catharsis. It is worth noting that this closet drama has a pendant in a shorter scene in a public toilet in the story "Franny" which misled many *New Yorker* readers into thinking that Franny was pregnant—why else, having left her boy friend at the table, was she shutting herself up in a toilet in the ladies' room, hanging her head and feeling sick?

Those readers were not "in" on the fact that Franny was having a mystical experience. Sex, which commonly takes two, not related by blood, is an experience that does not seem to possess erotic interest (phonies do it) for Salinger, and Zooey behind the shower curtain is taboo even to the mother who bore him. He is separated from her, as in a temple, by a veil. The reader, however, is allowed an extended look.

A great deal of attention is paid too to the rituals of cigarette lighting and of drinking from a glass, as though these oral acts were sacred—epiphanies. In the same way, the family writings are treated by Salinger as sacred scriptures or the droppings of holy birds, to be studied with care by the augurs: letters from Seymour, citations from his diary, a letter from Buddy, a letter from Franny, a letter from Boo Boo, a note written by Boo Boo in soap on a bathroom mirror (the last two are from another story, "Raise High the Roof Beam, Carpenters").

These imprints of the Glass collective personality are preserved as though they were Veronica's veil in a relic case of well-wrought prose. And the eerie thing is, speaking of Veronica's veil—a popular subject for those paintings in which Christ's eyes are supposed to follow the spectator with a doubtless reproachful gaze—the reader has the sensation in this latest work of Salinger that the author is sadly watching him or listening to him read. That is, the ordinary relation is reversed, and instead of the reader reading Salinger, Salinger, that Man of Sorrows, is reading the reader.

At the same time, this quasi-religious volume is full of Broadway humor. The Glass family is like a Jewish family in a radio serial. Everyone is a "character." Mr. Glass with his tangerine is a character; Mrs. Glass in her hairnet and commodious wrapper with her cups of chicken broth is a character. The shower curtain, scarlet nylon with a design of canary-yellow sharps, clefs, and flats, is a character; the teeming medicine cabinet is a character. Every phonograph, every chair is a character. The family relationship, rough, genial, insulting, is a character.

In short, every single object possessed by the Glass communal ego is bent on lovably expressing the Glass personality —eccentric, homey, goodhearted. Not unlike *Abie's Irish Rose*. And the family is its own best audience. Like Hemingway stooges, they have the disturbing faculty of laughing delightedly or smiling discreetly at each other's jokes. Again a closed circuit: the Glass family is the Fat Lady, who is Jesus. The mirrored Glass medicine cabinet is Jesus, and Seymour is his prophet.

Yet below this self-loving barbershop harmony a chord of terror is struck from time to time, like a judgment. Seymour's suicide suggests that Salinger guesses intermittently or fears intermittently that there may be something wrong somewhere. Why did he kill himself? Because he had married a phony, whom he worshiped for her "simplicity, her terrible honesty"? Or because he was so happy and the Fat Lady's world was so wonderful?

Or because he had been lying, his author had been lying, and it was all terrible, and he was a fake?

October, 1962

Burroughs' *Naked Lunch*

LAST summer at the International Writers' Conference in Edinburgh, I said I thought the national novel, like the nation-state, was dying and that a new kind of novel, based on state-lessness, was beginning to be written. This novel had a high, aerial point of view and a plot of perpetual motion. Two experiences, that of exile and that of jet-propelled mass tourism, provided the subject matter for a new kind of story. There is no novel, yet, that I know of, about mass tourism, but somebody will certainly write it. Of the novel based on stateless-ness, I gave as examples William Burroughs' *The Naked Lunch*, Vladimir Nabokov's *Pale Fire* and *Lolita*. Burroughs, I explained, is not literally a political exile, but the drug addicts he describes are continually on the move, and life in the United States, with its present narcotics laws, is untenable for the addict if he does not want to spend it in jail (in the same way, the confirmed homosexual is a chronic refugee, ordered to move on by the Venetian police, the Capri police, the mayor of Provincetown, the mayor of Nantucket). Had I read it at the time, I might have added Günter Grass's *The Tin Drum* to the list: here the point of view, instead of being high, is very low—that of a dwarf; the hero and narrator is a displaced person, born in the Free City of Danzig, of a Polish mother (who is not really a Pole but a member of a minority within Poland) and an uncertain father, who may be a German grocer or a Polish postal employee. In any case, I said

42

that in thinking over the novels of the last few years, I was struck by the fact that the only ones that had not simply given me pleasure but interested me had been those of Burroughs and Nabokov. The others, even when well done (Compton-Burnett), seemed almost regional.

This statement, to judge by the British press, was a shot heard round the world. I still pick up its reverberations in Paris and read about them in the American press. I am quoted as saying that *The Naked Lunch* is the most important novel of the age, of the epoch, of the century. The only truthful report of what I said about Burroughs was given by Stephen Spender in *Encounter,* October 1962. But nobody seems to have paid attention to Spender any more than anyone paid attention to what I said on the spot. When I chided Malcolm Muggeridge in person with having terribly misquoted me in the *New Statesman,* he appeared to think that there was not much difference between saying that a book was one of two or three that had interested you in the last few years and saying that it was one of the "outstanding novels of the age." According to me, the age is still Proust, Joyce, Kafka, Lawrence, Faulkner, to mention only the "big names," but to others evidently the age is shrinking to the length of a publishing season, just as a literary speaker is turned into a publisher's tout. The result, of course, is a disparagement of Burroughs, because if *The Naked Lunch* is proclaimed as the masterpiece of the century, then it is easily found wanting. Indeed, I wonder whether the inflation of my remarks was not at bottom malicious; it is not usually those who admire Burroughs who come up to me at parties to announce: "I *read* what you said at Edinburgh." This is true, I think, of all such publicity; it is malicious in effect whatever the intention and permits the reader to dismiss works of art and public figures as "not what they are cracked up to be." A similar thing happened with *Dr. Zhivago,* a wonderful book, which attracted much hatred and venom because it was not Tolstoy. Very few critics said it was Tolstoyan, but the impression got around that they had. Actually, as I recall, the critics who mentioned Tolstoy in connection with Pasternak were those bent on destroying Pasternak's book.

As for me, I was left in an uncomfortable situation. I did not want to write to the editors of British newspapers and magazines, denying that I had said whatever incontinent thing they had quoted me as saying. This would have been ungracious to Burroughs, who was the innocent party in the affair and who must have felt more and more like the groom in a shotgun literary wedding, seeing my name yoked with his as it were indissolubly. And the monstrousness of the union, doubtless, was what kept the story hot. In the end, it became clear to me that the only way I could put an end to this embarrassment was by writing at length what I thought about *The Naked Lunch*—something I was reluctant to do because I was busy finishing a book of my own and reluctant, also, because the whole thing had assumed the proportions of a *cause célèbre* and I felt like a witness called to the stand and obliged to tell the truth and nothing but the truth under oath. This is not a normal critical position. Of course the critic normally tries to be truthful, but he does not feel that his review is some sort of pay-off or eternal reckoning, that the eye of God or the world press is staring into his heart as he writes. Now that I have written the present review, I am glad, as always happens, to have made a clean breast of it. This is what I think about Burroughs.

"You can cut into *The Naked Lunch* at any intersection point," says Burroughs, suiting the action to the word, in "an atrophied preface" he appends as a tailpiece. His book, he means, is like a neighborhood movie with continuous showings that you can drop into whenever you please—you don't have to wait for the beginning of the feature picture. Or like a worm that you can chop up into sections each of which wriggles off as an independent worm. Or a nine-lived cat. Or a cancer. He is fond of the word "mosaic," especially in its scientific sense of a plant-mottling caused by a virus, and his Muse (see etymology of "mosaic") is interested in organic processes of multiplication and duplication. The literary notion of time as simultaneous, a montage, is not original with Burroughs; what is original is the scientific bent he gives it and a view of the world that combines biochemistry, anthropology, and politics. It is as though *Finnegans Wake* were cut loose from history and adapted for a Cinerama circus titled "One World." *The Naked Lunch* has no use for history, which is all "ancient history"—sloughed-off skin; from its planetary perspective, there are only geography and customs. Seen in terms of space, history shrivels into a mere wrinkling or furrowing of the surface as in an aerial relief-map or one of those pieced-together aerial photographs known in the trade as (again) mosaics. The oldest memory in *The Naked Lunch* is of jacking-off in boyhood latrines, a memory recaptured through pederasty. This must be the first space novel, the first serious piece of science fiction—the others are entertainment.

The action of *The Naked Lunch* takes place in the consciousness of One Man, William Lee, who is taking a drug cure. The principal characters, besides Lee, are his friend, Bill Gains (who seems momentarily to turn into a woman called Jane); various members of the Narcotic Squad, especially one Bradley the Buyer; Dr. Benway, a charlatan medico who is treating Lee; two vaudevillians, Clem and Jody; A. J., a carnival con man, the last of the Big Spenders; a sailor; an Arab called Ahmed; an archetypal Southern druggist, Doc Parker ("a man don't have no secrets from God and his druggist"); and various boys with whining voices. Among the minor characters are a number of automobiles, each with its specific complaint, like the oil-burning Ford V-8; a film executive; the Party Leader; the Vigilante; John and Mary, the sex acrobats; and a puzzled American housewife who is heard complaining because the Mixmaster keeps trying to climb up under her dress. The scene shifts about, from New York to Chicago to St. Louis to New Orleans to Mexico to Malmö, Tangier, Venice, and the human identities shift about too, for all these modern places and modern individuals (if that is the right word) have interchangeable parts. Burroughs is fond too of the word "ectoplasm," and the beings that surround Lee, particularly the inimical ones, seem ectoplasmic phantoms projected on the wide screen of his consciousness from a mass séance. But the haunting is less visual than auditory. These "characters," in the colloquial sense, are ventriloquial voices produced, as it were, against the will of the ventriloquist, who has become their dummy. Passages of dialogue and description keep recurring in different contexts with slight variations, as though they possessed ubiquity.

The best comparison for the book, with its aerial sex acts performed on a high trapeze, its con men and barkers, its arena-like form, is in fact with a circus. A circus travels but it is always the same, and this is Burroughs' sardonic image of modern life. The Barnum of the show is the mass-manipulator, who appears in a series of disguises. *Control,* as Burroughs says, underlining it, *can never be a means to anything but more control—like drugs,* and the vicious circle of addiction is re-enacted, worldwide, with sideshows in the political and "social" sphere—the "social" here has vanished, except in quotation marks, like the historical, for everything has become automatized. Everyone is an addict of one kind or another, as people indeed are wont to say of themselves, complacently: "I'm a crossword puzzle addict, a hi-fi addict," etc. The South is addicted to lynching and nigger-hating, and the Southern folk-custom of burning a Negro recurs throughout the book as a sort of Fourth-of-July carnival with fireworks. Circuses, with their cages of wild animals, are also dangerous, like Burroughs' human circus; an accident may occur, as when the electronic brain in Dr. Benway's laboratory goes on the rampage, and the freaks escape to mingle with the controlled citizens of Freeland in a general riot, or in the scene where the hogs are let loose in the gourmet restaurant.

On a level usually thought to be "harmless," addiction to platitudes and commonplaces is global. To Burroughs' ear, the Bore, lurking in the hotel lobby, is literally deadly (" 'You look to me like a man of intelligence.' Always ominous opening words, my boy!"). The same for Doc Parker with his captive customer in the back room of his pharmacy (". . . so long as you got a legitimate condition and an RX from a certified bona feedy M.D., I'm honored to serve you"), the professor in the classroom ("Hehe hehe he"), the attorney in court ("Hehe hehe he," likewise). The complacent sound of snickering laughter is an alarm signal, like the suave bell-tones of the psychiatrist and the emphatic drone of the Party Leader ("You see men and women. *Ordinary* men and women going about their ordinary everyday tasks. Leading their ordinary lives. That's what we need . . .").

Cut to ordinary men and women, going about their ordinary everyday tasks. The whine of the put-upon boy hustler: "All kinda awful sex acts." "Why cancha just get physical like a human?" "So I guess he come to some kinda awful climax." "You think I am innarested to hear about your horrible old condition? I am not innarested at all." "But he comes to a climax and turns into some kinda awful crab." This aggrieved tone merges with the malingering sighs of the American housewife, opening a box of Lux: "I got the most awful cold, and my intestines is all constipated." And the clarion of the Salesman: "When the Priority numbers are called up yonder I'll be there." These average folks are addicts of the science page of the Sunday supplements; they like to talk about their diseases and about vile practices that paralyze the practitioner from the waist down or about a worm that gets into your kidney and grows to enormous size or about the "horrible" result of marijuana addiction—it makes you turn black and your legs drop off. The superstitious scientific vocabulary is diffused from the laboratory and the mental hospital into the general population. Overheard at a lynching: "Don't crowd too close, boys. His intestines is subject to explode in the fire." The same diffusion of culture takes place with modern physics. A lieutenant to his general: "But chief, can't we get them started and they imitate each other like a chained reaction?"

The phenomenon of repetition, of course, gives rise to boredom; many readers complain that they cannot get through *The Naked Lunch*. And/or that they find it disgusting. It *is* disgusting and sometimes tiresome, often in the same places. The prominence of the anus, of faeces, and of all sorts of "horrible" discharges, as the characters would say, from the body's orifices, becomes too much of a bad thing, like the sado-masochistic sex performances—the auto-ejaculation of a hanged man is not everybody's cantharides. A reader whose erogenous zones are more temperate than the author's begins to feel either that he is a square (a guilty sentiment he should not yield to) or that he is the captive of a joyless addict.

In defense, Swift could be cited, and indeed between Burroughs and Swift there are many points of comparison; not only the obsession with excrement and the horror of female genitalia but a disgust with politics and the whole body politic. Like Swift, Burroughs has irritable nerves and something of the crafty temperament of the inventor. There is a great deal of Laputa in the countries Burroughs calls Interzone and Freeland, and Swift's solution for the Irish problem would appeal to the American's dry logic. As Gulliver, Swift posed as an anthropologist (though the study was not known by that name then) among savage people; Burroughs parodies the anthropologist in his descriptions of the American heartland: ". . . the Interior a vast subdivision, antennae of television to the meaningless sky . . . Illinois and Missouri, miasma of mound-building peoples, groveling worship of the Food Source, cruel and ugly festivals." The style here is more emotive than Swift's, but in his deadpan explanatory notes ("This is a rural English custom designed to eliminate aged and bedfast dependents"), there is a Swiftian laconic factuality. The "factual" appearance of the whole narrative, with its battery of notes and citations, some straight, some loaded, its extracts from a diary, like a ship's log, its pharmacopoeia, has the flavor of eighteenth-century satire. He calls himself a "Factualist" and belongs, all alone, to an Age of Reason, which he locates in the future. In him, as in Swift, there is a kind of soured utopianism.

Yet what saves *The Naked Lunch* is not a literary ancestor but humor. Burroughs' humor is peculiarly American, at once broad and sly. It is the humor of a comedian, a vaudeville performer playing in "One," in front of the asbestos curtain of some Keith Circuit or Pantages house long since converted to movies. The same jokes reappear, slightly refurbished, to suit the circumstances, the way a vaudeville artist used to change Yonkers to Renton when he was playing Seattle. For example, the Saniflush joke, which is always good for a laugh: somebody is cutting the cocaine/the morphine/the penicillin with Saniflush. Some of the jokes are verbal ("Stop me if you've heard this atomic secret" or Dr. Benway's "A simopath . . . is a citizen convinced he is an ape or other simian. It is a disorder peculiar to the army and discharge cures it"). Some are "black" parody (Dr. Benway, in his last appearance, dreamily, his voice fading out: "Cancer, my first love"). Some are whole vaudeville "numbers," as when the hoofers, Clem and Jody, are hired by the Russians to give Americans a bad name abroad: they appear in Liberia wearing black Stetsons and red galluses and talking loudly about burning niggers back home. A skit like this may rise to a frenzy, as if in a Marx Brothers or a Clayton, Jackson, and Durante act, when all the actors pitch in. *E.g.,* the very funny scene in Chez Robert, "where a huge icy gourmet broods over the greatest cuisine in the world": A. J. appears, the last of the Big Spenders, and orders a bottle of ketchup; immediate pandemonium; A. J. gives his hog-call, and the shocked gourmet diners are all devoured by famished hogs. The effect of pandemonium, all hell breaking loose, is one of Burroughs' favorites and an equivalent of the old vaudeville finale, with the acrobats, the jugglers, the magician, the hoofers, the lady-who-was-sawed-in-two, the piano-player, the comedians, all pushing into the act.

Another favorite effect, with Burroughs, is the metamorphosis. A citizen is turned into animal form, a crab or a huge centipede, or into some unspeakable monstrosity, like Bradley the Narcotics Agent who turns into an unidentifiable carnivore. These metamorphoses, of course, are punishments. The Hellzapoppin effect of orgies and riots and the metamorphosis effect, rapid or creeping, are really cancerous onslaughts—matter on the rampage multiplying itself and "building" as a revue scene "builds" to a climax. Growth and deterioration are the same thing: a human being "deteriorates" or grows into a one-man jungle. What you think of it depends on your point of view; from the junky's angle, Bradley is better as a carnivore eating the Narcotics Commissioner than he was as "fuzz"—junky slang for the police.

The Naked Lunch contains messages that unluckily for the ordinary reader are somewhat arcane. Despite his irony, Burroughs is a prescriptive writer. He means what he says to be taken and used literally, like an Rx prescription. Unsentimental and factual, he writes as though his thoughts had the quality of self-evidence. In a special sense, *The Naked Lunch* is coterie literature. It was not intended, surely, for the general public, but for addicts and former addicts, with the object of imparting information. Like a classical satirist, Burroughs is dead serious—a reformer. Yet, as often happened with the classical satirists, a wild hilarity and savage pessimism carry him beyond his therapeutic purpose and defeat it. The book is alive, like a basketful of crabs, and common sense cannot get hold of it to extract a moral.

On the one hand, control is evil; on the other, escape from control is mass slaughter or reduction to a state of proliferating cellular matter. The police are the enemy, but as Burroughs shrewdly observes in one passage: "A *functioning* police state needs no police." The policeman is internalized in the robotized citizen. From a libertarian point of view, nothing could be worse. This would seem to be Burroughs' position, but it is not consistent with his picture of sex. To be a libertarian in politics implies a faith in Nature and the natural, that is, in the life-principle itself, commonly identified with sex. But there is little affection for the life-principle in *The Naked Lunch,* and sex, while magnified—a common trait of homosexual literature—is a kind of mechanical man-trap baited with fresh meat. The sexual climax, the jet of sperm, accompanied by a whistling scream, is often a death spasm, and the "perfect" orgasm would seem to be the posthumous orgasm of the hanged man, shooting his jism into pure space.

It is true that Nature and sex are two-faced, and that growth is death-oriented. But if Nature is not seen as far more good than evil, then a need for control is posited. And, strangely, this seems to be Burroughs' position too. *The human virus can now be treated,* he says with emphasis, meaning the species itself. By scientific methods, he implies. Yet the laboratory of *The Naked Lunch* is a musical-comedy inferno, and Dr. Benway's assistant is a female chimpanzee. As Burroughs knows, the Men in White, when not simple con men, are the fuzz in another uniform.

The Naked Lunch, Burroughs says, is "a blueprint, a How-To Book. . . . How-To extend levels of experience by opening the door at the end of a long hall." Thus the act of writing resembles and substitutes for drug-taking, which in Burroughs' case must have begun as an experiment in the extension of consciousness. It does not sound as if pleasure had ever been his motive. He was testing the controls of his own mechanism to adjust the feed-in of data, noting with care the effects obtained from heroin, morphine, opium, Demerol, Yage, cannabis, and so on. These experiments, aiming at freedom, "opening a door," resulted in addiction. He kicked the imprisoning habit by what used to be known as will power, supplemented by a non-addictive drug, apomorphine, to whose efficacy he now writes testimonials. It seems clear that what was involved and continues to be involved for Burroughs is a Faustian compact: knowledge-as-power, total control of the self, which is experienced as sovereign in respect to the immediate environment and neutral in respect to others.

At present he is interested in scientology, which offers its initiates the promise of becoming "clears"—free from all hang-ups. For the novel he has invented his cut-out and fold-in techniques, which he is convinced can rationalize the manufacture of fictions by applying modern factory methods to the old "writer's craft." A text may be put together by two or three interested and moderately skilled persons equipped with scissors and the raw material of a typescript. Independence from the vile body and its "algebra of need," freedom of movement across national and psychic frontiers, efficiency of work and production, by means of short cuts, suppression of connectives, and other labor-saving devices, would be Uncle Bill Burroughs' patent for successful living. But if such a universal passkey can really be devised, what is its purpose? It cannot be enjoyment of the world, for this would only begin the addictive process all over again by creating dependency. Action, the reverse of enjoyment, has no appeal either for the author of *The Naked Lunch*. What Burroughs wants is out, which explains the dry, crankish amusement given him by space, interplanetary distances, where, however, he finds the old mob still at work. In fact, his reasoning, like the form of his novel, is circular. Liberation leads to new forms of subjugation. If the human virus can be treated, this can only be under conditions of asepsis: the Nova police. Yet Burroughs is unwilling, politically, to play the dread game of eugenics or euthenics, outside his private fantasy, which, since his intelligence is aware of the circularity of its utopian reasoning, invariably turns sardonic. *Quis custodet custodes ipsos?*

March, 1963

The Hue and Cry

WHEN I read *Eichmann in Jerusalem* in *The New Yorker* last winter I thought it splendid and extraordinary. I still do. But apparently this is because I am a Gentile. As a Gentile, I don't "understand." Neither do any of my Gentile friends and relations, who speak about it to me in lowered voices. "Did *you* get that out of it?" "No." The only Gentiles who have "understood" in print have been rather special cases: Judge Musmanno, who was attacked in the book, Professor Trevor-Roper, who has a corner on Nazi history in its popular form, and Richard Crossman, M.P., who has been championing the state of Israel since 1946 and who winters in Tiberias.* So far as I know, all Miss Arendt's hostile reviews, not counting these, have come from Jews, and those favorable to her from Gentiles, with four exceptions: A. Alvarez, George Lichtheim, Bruno Bettelheim, and Daniel Bell. The division between Jew and Gentile is even more pronounced in private

* The name of John Sparrow, Warden of All Souls, could now be added to the list of Gentiles who attacked Miss Arendt. His unsigned review came out in the London *Times Literary Supplement,* after my article was written, and included me in the attack. Anybody interested in studying this controversy is referred to *Partisan Review,* Summer 1963, Fall 1963, and Spring 1964. He will find articles and letters, pro and con, by Lionel Abel, Marie Syrkin, Daniel Bell, Irving Howe, Robert Lowell, William Phillips, and Harold Weisberg. My own piece, an answer mainly to Abel, appeared in the Winter 1964 number. Since it is part of a now historical debate, I have made only minute revisions.

54

conversation, where a Gentile, once the topic is raised in Jewish company (and it always is), feels like a child with a reading defect in a class of normal readers—or the reverse. It is as if *Eichmann in Jerusalem* had required a special pair of Jewish spectacles to make its "true purport" visible. And such propagandists as Lionel Abel, writing in *Partisan Review* (Summer 1963), and Marie Syrkin, writing in *Dissent,* have been eagerly offering their pair to the reader for a peep into Miss Arendt's mind. "The Clothes of the Empress" Miss Syrkin calls her review, advertising a display of Miss Arendt seen through, exposed in all her nakedness. In a cruder way, her antagonists in private "expose" her as an anti-Semite, and a newspaper story speaks of the wife of an Israeli official in New York who kept calling her "Hannah Eichmann"—by a slip of the tongue, of course. More moderate parlor critics talk of "arrogance"or "lack of proportion" in her treatment of the Jewish Councils while conceding that Miss Arendt is of course not an anti-Semite or an admirer of Eichmann's. But this is said in the tone of a *concession;* these Jews, many of whom call themselves friends of the author, are more interested in enumerating the shortcomings of her book than in repelling the slanders that are circulating about her in and out of print. These slanders, which they hear all the time and which are intended to destroy the reputation of a living woman, excite them far less than Miss Arendt's "slander" of the Jewish leadership, who are dead and beyond being hurt by it, if it *is* a slander. I am told that at a meeting held under the auspices of *Dissent* to discuss Miss Arendt's book only one voice from the audience was raised in her defense and that voice was shouted down; some others present including Jews disagreed with what was being said but they remained silent.*

In such an atmosphere, so remote from that of free speech,

* A different version of this episode was given by Irving Howe in a letter to the magazine, Spring 1964.

Partisan Review published Lionel Abel's "The Aesthetics of Evil," with the announcement that it was opening a discussion. In other words, Miss Arendt's defenders would be given an opportunity to reply. Daniel Bell's very good piece in the last issue was not so much a defense as a plea for an armistice, so I am going to speak up, but it is with a heavy heart. First because I am Miss Arendt's friend, and friends are regarded as prejudiced. Second because I am a Gentile, and I fear that this fact will only rejoice her enemies, since are not all Gentiles anti-Semitic? Third because I do not feel that Abel's piece deserves a reply on its own merits. I can only see it as a document in a hate campaign against Miss Arendt and one of the worst. The two serious points Abel raises—a) how does Miss Arendt account for the mass slaughter of Jews in the Ukraine when no Jewish organizations existed there? b) how does she reconcile her criticism of the Jewish leadership with the picture of totalitarian terror she gave in *The Origins of Totalitarianism?*—are so entwined with insinuations, innuendoes, charges of bad faith that it is hard to free the trunk of his argument from this mass of creepers and look at it squarely. He accuses Miss Arendt throughout of deliberately suppressing evidence ("She must know very well," etc.) that does not suit her hand, and he nudges the reader to guess what that "hand" may be: infatuation with her own ideas, a love-hate affair with totalitarianism, a preference for butchers over their victims, for the strong over the weak, for—why not say it?—the Nazis over the Jews. As a reader, Abel claims to feel that Eichmann "comes off so much better in the book than his victims." This is given a priori, though it is also his conclusion, which is arrived at by a vicious circle—the term never sounded more apt. "Eichmann is aesthetically palatable, and his victims are aesthetically repulsive," he finishes, as he began. He offers no evidence on behalf of this idea. He can defend it, if he wishes, as his personal impression. But this is more of a judgment of Abel than of Miss Arendt: reading her book, he liked Eichmann better than the Jews who died in the crematoriums. Each to his own taste. It was not my impression.

But since Abel is not the only one to insist that Eichmann somehow got preferential treatment, he must be answered, if only as a spokesman for those less well read and less intellectually gifted than he. It is hardly credible to me that any reader, no matter how stupid, could really imagine that Miss Arendt divides the guilt equally between Eichmann and the Jews, let alone that she regards Eichmann as a lovely object in contrast to the Jewish dead. And yet this has happened, and it must be understood.

Before writing this, I have gone back and reread *Eichmann in Jerusalem* as objectively as I can. My original feeling was that the part allotted to the Jewish leadership was quite small in the whole story Miss Arendt told. It had not struck me particularly, especially since it was not new; anybody who had followed the Kastner case or had read reviews of the Hilberg book was familiar with the fact of Jewish co-operation; such co-operation, indeed, was only another facet of the story told in concentration-camp literature by Rousset, Margarete Buber-Neumann, Bettelheim, and others: the leaders of the victims co-operated with their jailers. My original feeling proved to be right: in a book of two hundred and sixty pages, eight pages are devoted to the co-operation of the Jewish leadership with Eichmann's office, and two and a quarter pages to a discussion of privileged categories of Jews (war veterans, famous people, etc.). Both passages are certainly critical, and the second, which reviews the conduct not only of Jews but of Gentile groups in pressing the Nazis for "special" treatment for special Jews, seems to me harsher. Besides this there are passing references to Jewish co-operation or the lack of it.

Now some of Miss Arendt's critics complain that she gave too much space and prominence to this topic (how can one measure prominence?), while others, including Abel, say that her treatment was too short. The only way to have satisfied both parties would have been to omit the whole subject, which is probably what most Jews would have liked best. My conclusion is that those who were truly shocked and pained by these "revelations" were not shocked and pained by the fact (which they must have known about at least vaguely) but by the context in which it was put. Miss Arendt's boldness was putting this distressing material in the context of the Nazi guilt, where Jews felt it did not belong, where it was "out of all proportion." To speak in the same breath of the guilt of Eichmann and the guilt of the *Judenräte* seemed offensive, like equating them; yet Miss Arendt never for one instant equates them, and how could she assess the activities of Eichmann while suppressing the part played by the Jewish leaders, with whom his office constantly dealt?

When she writes her famous sentence (often distorted in quotation), "To a Jew this role of the Jewish leaders in the destruction of their own people is undoubtedly the darkest chapter of the whole dark story," she is expressing the same pain her Jewish readers felt in reading her summary of that "dark chapter" and for which they are ready to condemn her, as a tyrant used to condemn to death the messenger of bad news. The "darkest chapter," incidentally, does not mean the worst; it means the hardest to contemplate, for a Jew.

As for Abel's contention that she ought to have discussed the motives and arguments of the Jewish leaders, she indicates that these motives ranged from high to low, as one would expect. Abel's imagination was demonstrably quite able to reconstruct the arguments that must have taken place —a feat not beyond the power of the ordinary reader. Possibly what some Jews feared was that though they themselves could understand these motives, others (Gentiles?) might not. What many of her critics hold against her is that she tried to understand Eichmann and does not make the same effort for the Jewish leaders. But their behavior is quite understandable, unlike that of the Nazis. They acted the way most respectable citizens would; they temporized, tried not to think the worst, looked for a formula that would placate the enemy. The name of this in politics is appeasement. Miss Arendt, says Abel, does not mention the middle-class character of the Jewish Councils. She did not have to.

Abel claims that Miss Arendt blames the leadership for not having resisted. She does not. The question of resistance is raised on pages nine and ten of her book. Her conclusion is that resistance was impossible. But between resistance and co-operation there was a small space in which some action—or, rather, resolution—might have been taken. Miss Arendt perhaps exaggerates the size of this space, and it must have varied from country to country and town to town. The example she gives of the Danish rabbi who called his people together, told them the truth, that an order had gone out for their deportation, and ordered them to disperse, no doubt would have been impossible to follow with success in countries where the native population was hostile and physically and culturally distinct from the Jews, but in some places, at some times, it could have been followed. Miss Arendt's other famous sentence, that without the co-operation of the Jewish Councils four and a half to six million Jews would not have perished, seems to me almost self-evidently true. Had the Nazis been obliged to use their own manpower to select Jews for the extermination camps, number them, assemble them, ticket their property, and so on, they would not only have rounded up fewer Jews, but they would have felt the drain in their military effort; had Hitler persisted in the Final Solution, at the cost of diverting troops to carry it out, the war might have ended somewhat sooner. It is clear that refusal to co-operate would have met with terrible reprisals, but these reprisals in turn might have demoralized the army and the civilian population both in Germany and in the occupied countries, and chaos, the nightmare of generals, might have been the result. The Final Solution was preferred by the Nazis to mass execution by shooting because it could be carried out smoothly and efficiently—almost peacefully. And this allowed not only the Germans and the people of the occupied countries but the Jews themselves for a long time to remain ignorant of the true destination of the cattle cars moving east, on schedule. To say this is not—horrible charge—to "desire to maximize the role of Jewish leaders in the destruction of European Jewry." Nor is it to show a lack of sympathy for their plight. To speculate on the past, as Abel ought to know, is not to blame (it is too late for that), but merely to wish, to regret, to close your eyes and see it done differently, in some cases to admire.

Smoothly and efficiently—almost peacefully. This was the fearful characteristic of the Final Solution, and for this Eichmann, the transportation expert, was the perfect instrument. Of course six psychiatrists pronounced him normal; he *was* normal and average and therefore perfectly fitted for his job, which was to "make the wheels run smoothly," in both a literal and figurative sense. His function was to normalize the Final Solution. With his conceit and boasting, his pompous home-made clichés and "winged words," he was at once ridiculous and ordinary, for ordinariness carried to a zenith is absurd. No better example of the mass murderer who is at the same time a perfect family man (Chaplin's Monsieur Verdoux) could be found than the ineffable Eichmann. One of his lawyers said he was like a mailman—a person you see every day on his methodical rounds and seldom notice. Naturally he got along well with Jews; it was part of his job to do so. Among the clichés he incorporated in his personality (to speak of his "character" would be a mistake) was the Some-of-my-best-friends cliché. That he could push this to the point of imagining that he had been converted to Zionism (the Jewish Final Solution) was pushing the logic of the cliché to the nth degree of complacency and self-delusion. How could Abel have missed the irony in Miss Arendt's account of his "conversion"—a dramatic irony, furthermore, since when she tells the reader that Eichmann had been "promptly and forever" made a Zionist by reading a "basic book," she is dryly summing up a speaker who had no idea of the effect on an audience of what he was saying? It was Eichmann, alone in the world, who considered himself a good disciple of Herzl.

According to Abel, Eichmann must have thought about Nazism politically since he thought about Zionism. But Eichmann's "thought" was a parody of the idea of thinking. Had *Mein Kampf* been his "Bible," he might have pressed a flower in it. His Zionist "studies" had a function; they made him an expert, at least in the circles he moved in. They made him "stand out" from his co-workers—the life-object of all mediocrities. As a specialist in Jewish emigration, he was perfectly fitted, when the time came, to arrange Jewish emigration to the next world, to Abraham's bosom. Among his fellow-bureaucrats, he might have passed highest in a vocational aptitude test for the new job. A sadist, monster, or demon would not have qualified for the position; these "undesirables" had their place in the Nazi system as jailers and editors of periodicals, but a man with Eichmann's responsibilities could not be a Beast of Belsen or a Julius Streicher. The fact that Eichmann was squeamish, could not bear the sight of blood, was even an "idealist" permitted precisely that distancing from reality that facilitated the administrative task—a distancing that reflected the physical and psychic space between the collective will of the German people in the homeland and its execution in the east. If Eichmann seems to have been cordial, rather than the block of ice described by one witness, this was good public relations, for one of his duties was to allay the suspicions of the Jews and other foreigners he came in contact with, so that they too would be distanced from reality.

Abel does not think that Miss Arendt should have assigned dutifulness—"a positive value"—to Eichmann, as though she were free, reporting the trial, to invent her own Eichmann like a character in fiction. I should have thought dutifulness was a relative value. But in any case the picture of Eichmann as a conscientious clown emerged from Eichmann's testimony long before Miss Arendt wrote her book. Miss Arendt's achievement was to reconcile this virtuous clown with his actions. The portrait she made, of course, is not the "final" Eichmann—there can be no such thing—and some day someone may square the man as he appeared with his actions in some entirely different way. But none of her critics has even tried to do this. To say that he was a monster does not meet the problem, unless a monster means someone you cannot explain, which is to declare the problem insoluble. Perhaps Abel thinks Eichmann was a play-actor?

It strikes me now that one of Miss Arendt's offenses was to put Eichmann together with what he did, not in terms of rhetoric, but on a realistic basis, listening to him and watching him—as though this in itself were dangerous, as though the trite proverb, which one can imagine in Eichmann's mouth (for did he not seek his judges' "understanding," by which he must have meant acquittal?), were an established truth and to try to understand Eichmann were to forgive him. Understanding is often a prelude to forgiveness, but they are not the same, and we often forgive what we cannot understand (seeing nothing else to do) and understand what we cannot pardon. Miss Arendt does not forgive Eichmann; indeed she unequivocally passes the death sentence on him herself, in her last paragraph—an act which may appear arrogant or which may appear as the resolute shouldering of the task of judging, *i.e.,* the taking of responsibility, which Eichmann himself al-

ways shrank from and in which he revealed his squeamish-
ness and mediocrity.

What satisfaction would it have given Abel and others if
Miss Arendt had accepted the word "monster" from the prosecutor's lips? Calling someone a monster does not make him
more guilty; it makes him less so by classing him with beasts
and devils ("a person of inhuman and horrible cruelty or
wickedness," OED, Sense 4). Such an unnatural being is
more horrible to contemplate than an Eichmann—that is,
aesthetically worse—but morally an Ilse Koch was surely
less culpable than Eichmann since she seems to have had no
trace of human feeling and therefore was impassible to conscience. Abel quotes a saying of Kierkegaard on Judas,
which shows Judas as comical, and he seems to think this
bears out his argument, since Judas, according to him, was a
monster. But Judas was not a monster, though his act was
monstrous; he was a man, the twelfth part of humanity, and
his sin was that he could betray for thirty pieces of silver, like
any common informer. Jesus was uncommon, not Judas. And
Judas, unlike a monster, knew that he had sinned and went
and hanged himself with a halter. Eichmann too knew himself
to be guilty somehow, somewhere ("before God," as he put
it), though he kept this knowledge in a separate pocket of his
mind, far from the actual trial, and was helped in this by the
prosecutor, who by charging him with acts of cruelty he did
not commit allowed him to feel innocent. What is horrible in
Eichmann *is* his ordinariness, including the prompt ability to
feel innocent when you are charged with a crime you did not
commit though you did something infinitely worse, like a person who is accused of murder and robbery and feels put upon
because it was not he who stole the victim's watch—he
"only" committed the murder.

But suppose this were just a quarrel about terms. Suppose
by "monster" Abel means someone capable of sending four
and a half to six million Jews to death. There is no argu-

ment if that is the definition—only a tautology. But if he means an exceptionally depraved and wicked creature, like Iago or Richard III (his examples), then it is he, it seems to me, who is building Eichmann up and making him an object of aesthetic interest.

The difficulty many people experienced in thinking about the Eichmann trial was to "make the punishment fit the crime." The desire of Abel and other critics is to make the criminal fit the crime. And just as any punishment seemed grotesquely small and insignificant beside the murder of millions of helpless people, so the criminal seemed grotesquely small and insignificant. This was not because he had shrunk in the interim. The disproportion between the doer and the deed is a disturbing fact of contemporary history—an effect of advanced technology, like automation. On the Allied side, you had Hiroshima and Nagasaki, where our boys in the bombers and Mr. Truman in the White House were simply incommensurable with what they had done. Not that Mr. Truman and Eichmann can be considered equally as mass murderers; Mr. Truman had a motive which at least was good —the quick ending of the war. It is just that the human scale is no longer in focus, and to measure an Eichmann by the number of his victims and his individual power by their multiplied helplessness is to magnify both him and it.

On the other hand, contrary to what Abel says, Miss Arendt never presents him as a "dutiful clerk"; his work was important, indeed crucial, in the Nazi scheme, and he could feel that he, as an individual, was making a significant contribution to the Fuehrer's task. He may or may not have conceived of himself as irreplaceable; if he did this was one of his delusions—a delusion no doubt shared by other Nazi functionaries, each of whom, on the lower levels, was replaceable while all of them together were not. Eichmann was free to quit his desk and his "great responsibilities" at any time, as Miss Arendt shows; no one forced him to do this particular work. Yet his staying on the job and the zeal he brought to it do not prove that he liked killing Jews, even at a distance. He liked being a functionary and "necessary," and if this entailed a certain amount of self-sacrifice he liked it even more, for he saw it in the preliminary terms Kant laid down in formulating the categorical imperative: that a virtuous action is one done against inclination. That an act done against inclination is therefore virtuous was Eichmann's mistaken understanding or perhaps his rationalization. As Miss Arendt sums up in a terrible flash of insight, "Evil in the Third Reich had lost the quality by which most people recognize it—the quality of temptation." In this passage, it seems to me, rereading her book, Miss Arendt's scorn and contempt for Eichmann were mingled with a kind of pained, wry-mouthed pity. Eichmann at this time—it was at the end of the war—was pressing for the continuation of the extermination policy, in obedience to the supreme "law" of the Fuehrer's will, long after many of his colleagues and superiors had seen the end coming and were seeking to save their skins by "saving" Jews. What she pities in Eichmann (if I do not misread her) is the extent to which he could go on doing evil when all careerist motives had disappeared and against his personal desires—to have stopped the transports to Auschwitz, in his blinkered view, would have been to yield to a temptation. If Abel wants a dramatic parallel for Eichmann, he ought to open his Ibsen. There he can find "idealists" as pernickety, as literal-minded, and nearly as dangerous to humanity. Like the simpletons in Ibsen who talk of the "demands of the ideal," Eichmann was a fool, and what is pitiable in the Eichmann Miss Arendt sees is his foolish consistency, the way in which his inner mechanism, his "soul," continued to tick like some trusty middle-class alarm clock, unaware that it had become an infernal machine and listening only to the sound of its own reliability, signifying that everything was normal.

And if Miss Arendt, a Jew, found it in her heart to pity

Eichmann, is this a sin? Is this "aesthetics"? To a Christian, it is ethics; can this be the Gentile "blind spot"? A Christian is commanded not only to pity but to forgive his enemies. It is a hard commandment, and if the Gentile reader detected Miss Arendt showing a trace of pity for the clown that had murdered her own people, he was not shocked but moved to admiration. Abel no doubt would say that she did not extend pity (or charity) to the Jewish leaders, but they were not in need of it to the same degree, any more than they were in need of a great effort of understanding. We all, including Miss Arendt, pity them in a natural motion of feeling, but this is not the pity that counts, ethically speaking, which goes not to those nearest to us (self-pity is scarcely a virtue) but to those farthest away and seemingly beyond the reach of human sympathy. Anybody can feel compassion for the Jewish leaders, even while criticizing their behavior. But "criticizing his behavior" is hardly what applies to Eichmann, and it would take a saint, as the saying goes, to feel pity for him.

To me, *Eichmann in Jerusalem,* despite all the horrors in it, was morally exhilarating. I freely confess that it gave me joy and I too heard a paean in it—not a hate-paean to totalitarianism but a paean of transcendence, heavenly music, like that of the final chorus of *Figaro* or the *Messiah.* As in these choruses, a pardon or redemption of some sort was taking place. The reader "rose above" the terrible material of the trial or was borne aloft to survey it with his intelligence. No person was pardoned, but the whole experience was bought back, redeemed, as in the harrowing of hell.

Now it is true that intelligence, mastering the incoherence of violence and suffering, gives it sense, *i.e.,* form, which is necessarily aesthetic. Miss Arendt's book tells a story. Here Abel's criticism just misses something real. Perhaps for Jews it is too soon to have what happened made into a story. They reject the idea that their sufferings made sense, had a plot and a lesson.

For me, however, the plot and the lesson were almost a godsend. For me as a reader, the episodes that stood out were those that dealt with the Jews who were saved—the happy endings. They were the redeeming features of an otherwise unbearable history: the stories of the Jews of Denmark, Bulgaria, and Italy. Possibly I liked them because the Gentiles behaved well in these chapters, but I think it was rather because these chapters showed that it was *possible* to behave well even in extreme situations, and it is worth noting that where the Gentiles behaved well, the Jews did not co-operate with the Nazi authorities. (An exception is Holland.) But I took the book mainly as a parable for the Gentiles in the widest sense of that word, *i.e.,* the innumerable "others," a lesson in what was possible for the average man, the neighbor, who is not *forced* to look the other way when the police cars come for the "Jews" next door—Jews figuratively speaking, since it might happen again, might be happening now, and the Jews of the past may not be the "Jews" of the present or the future. In this parable, as in all parables, there is a contrast. At one extreme there is Eichmann, who stands for all the Eichmanns in the Nazi bureaucracy, all the "little fellows" who asked after the event, "But what could we have done?" To them the Danes furnished an answer, which would have been the same if there had been only one Dane to wear the yellow star and he not a king but a "little fellow." In fact, the King of Denmark is not shown as a king but as the *other* neighbor, at the opposite pole from Eichmann. A whole range of neighbors, good and evil, is glimpsed through the trial in Jerusalem, one of the most evil being that Papal Nuncio in Hungary who passed on a protest to Horthy against the deportation of the Jews, adding that the Vatican's protest did not spring "from a false sense of compassion."

The parable did not speak, obviously, to the mass of Jews. But it spoke to privileged Jews, those with money and connections, for to the extent that privileged Jews were privileged, entitled to special treatment, endowed with power over others, they in effect were "Gentiles." The lesson, then, as I saw it, was addressed exclusively to the Gentiles, who were on trial through their representative, Eichmann. Some—a few —were exonerated, and no Jew, as a Jew, figured among the accused; the gassed Jews were the witnesses, bearing testimony for or against us.

No Gentile who was an adult in the years of the Final Solution can read *Eichmann in Jerusalem* without some remorse and self-questioning. American Jews, far from the scene then and now, may feel certain misgivings too, reading the book, especially the richer ones who paid large sums of money to the Nazis for the ransom of their relatives and did not concern themselves too greatly with the fate of "ordinary" Jews. Miss Arendt's harshness on this point may seem to them unkind and inappropriate in what they still think of as a time of mourning; it is like somebody who criticizes at a funeral. But the question is whether those who merely grieve for their fellow-beings show more compassion than those who in retrospect seek remedies, since to seek remedies implies a continuing concern that what happened shall never happen again. The State of Israel promises that to Jews, politically, by offering them a homeland, an army, and a foreign policy. "You are safe now," it tells them. Miss Arendt is not interested in the safety of Jews but in the safety of humanity. Trying to learn from history, she is thinking ahead on behalf of other "superfluous" people who may be the next "Jews" on someone's list for "resettlement in the east." Yet the official Israeli lesson supposedly taught by the trial—the need for a strong national state—is at very sharp variance with any parable for the Gentiles, *i.e.*, not only non-Jews but all the tribes and the peoples.

As a sample of moral fineness on the part of Miss Arendt's critics, I offer the following sentence from Abel's piece: "If a man holds a gun at the head of another and forces him to kill his friend, the man with the gun will be aesthetically less ugly than the one who out of fear of death has killed his friend and perhaps did not even save his own life." *Forces* him to kill his friend? Nobody by possession of a weapon can force a man to kill anybody; that is his own decision. If somebody points a gun at you and says "Kill your friend or I will kill you," he is *tempting* you to kill your friend. That is all.

I have already given some indication of Abel's morality as a critic, which permits him the free use of pseudo-paraphrase and downright invention. Now I have space for only three more examples. The first is the shifting use he makes of the word "victims." Miss Arendt criticizes the Jewish leadership; the Jewish leaders became victims; ergo, Miss Arendt criticizes the victims. The implication is that she is criticizing four and a half to six million innocent people. Second, he says he "wondered" when he read Miss Arendt's book why she did not deal with the killing of the Jews in the Ukraine. He did not wonder long; the reason was obvious to him: because this would have destroyed her whole thesis about the role of the Jewish leaders in the extermination of the Jews. She mentions several times the *Einsatzgruppen* shootings of the Jews in the Russian territories: they were shot on the spot together with Communist functionaries, Gypsies, criminals, and insane people. There were no Jewish organizations in Russia, but there were Jewish Councils in Poland, yet she does not deal with the extermination of Polish Jewry—a thing about which I wondered myself. But since I genuinely wondered, I was able to find a genuine answer on pages 197–198. The answer is Eichmann; he had nothing to do with the shootings in the East or with the gassing of Polish Jews or the management of Polish ghettoes. He was concerned with the logistics of supplying Jews to the death camps. Here too was where the Jewish Councils came in; they were, so to speak, Eichmann's draft board. Where the *Einsatzgruppen* shot masses of victims on the spot, there was no transportation problem, no question of selection, and no need for Jewish organizations, even if they had existed. The story of the Jews of the East was separate from the story of Eichmann, to which Miss Arendt restricted herself as much as possible.

An explanation, incidentally, of the ease with which not only Jews but other groups were rounded up and massacred in the Russian territories was offered me by a Polish friend. The Stalinist state apparatus had abolished all other social structures, and when it collapsed after the invasion, in the occupied territories there was nothing, a social void. It was impossible to hide, for there were no hiding-places—no convents, estates, private peasant farms. Most of the Jewish children who survived in Poland were hidden in convents, and villagers used to sell food to Jews hiding in the woods, which would have been impossible in a Russian collective, where everything was known. Stalin's totalitarian state had eliminated privacy.

Returning to Abel, here is the third example. "Why did Eichmann not suspect that the killing of so many defenseless persons was evil? This Miss Arendt never tries to explain." But he did suspect; he even knew, and this knowledge, his "conscience," lasted for about four weeks. Eichmann's conscience is the center of her book and explicitly the theme of several chapters. Clearly Abel is aware of this since he alludes to the subject himself, glancingly, in a typical misparaphrase: ". . . according to her view of what happened, the Jews of Europe were so compliant that Eichmann, their executioner, was even denied the opportunity to be conscience-stricken as he sent them off to die." What he says in this sentence is that Miss Arendt explains Eichmann's unsuspicious conscience by the compliancy of the Jews. She does not; the compliancy of the Jewish *leadership* (not the Jews) was one of the many factors she cites that contributed to the extinction of Eichmann's conscience, but the chief responsibility for this, as I read it, outside of Eichmann himself, lay with respectable German society, which remained almost totally silent at the time and only came forward later to wash its hands of the affair.

As the reader can see, the attempt to correct Abel on one point at once brings up another and leads, if one will let it, into a maze. It is like arguing with a hydra.

But I must at least touch on his final charge: the damning evidence he has discovered, where it was lying low, in *The Origins of Totalitarianism*. Frankly, I am not competent and do not have the time or space to get to the bottom of this. But supposing Abel is right and there is a contradiction between the earlier book and the present one, what would it prove? That she was right then and wrong now or vice versa? His triumphant tone seems to announce that she was wrong both times, which is impossible, at least in the terms in which he states her arguments—that the totalitarian state was "all-powerful" and that it was not. However, I do not think she said it was "all-powerful" and certainly would not take his word for it. In any case the passage he quotes is about totalitarian *terror,* not about the totalitarian state. And where the terror ruled—in the camps, prisons, and ghettoes—Miss Arendt does not propose that there was any choice but to obey.

To be fair, though, to Abel, it does seem to me that Miss Arendt's views about totalitarian rule are not as pessimistic as they were when Stalin was alive. But to change one's views somewhat, in the light of new evidence and new events (as she does in her chapters on Hungary in the new edition of *The Origins*), is a normal consequence of thought and does not call for you to "recant" or "retract." Unless Abel and those who agree with him are running a private Inquisition or police state.

Winter, 1964

On *Madame Bovary*

WHEN Flaubert made his famous statement—"Madame Bovary is me"—he was echoing one of his favorite authors, Cervantes. Cervantes, on his deathbed, so the story goes, was asked whom he meant to depict in Don Quixote. "Myself," he answered. In Cervantes' case, this must have been true, quite simply and terribly, whether or not he ever said it. In Flaubert's, the answer was an evasion. He was tired of being asked about the "real-life original" of his heroine. According to tradition, there *was* one; in fact, there may have been two or even three. First and most important was Delphine Delamare, née Couturier, the wife of a public-health officer in the Bray region of Normandy, not far from where Flaubert lived. In 1848, aged twenty-seven, she killed herself, leaving behind her a little girl, Alice-Delphine. Among her effects, it was said, was an unpaid bill from a circulating library in Rouen, Flaubert's friends had suggested her case to him as the subject for a novel, on the writing-course principle of "Write about what you know." What better source than a mother-in-law? Old Madame Delamare, the doctor's widowed mother, used to come to see old Madame Flaubert and lament his marital unhappiness, his untimely death; Flaubert's niece remembered her well and was convinced that the old lady's complaints about her daughter-in-law's misconduct were the basis for *Madame Bovary*. In an inventory of Delamare's property

72

and papers, made on his decease, an I.O.U. of three hundred francs to "Madame Flaubert" has recently been found.

Dr. Delamare had died, presumably of grief, like Charles Bovary, long before *Madame Bovary* appeared, in 1857; he survived his wife by only twenty-one months. But other principals in the Delamare drama (rumor gave her many lovers) and a chorus of commentators were still living. And many years later, in the village of Ry—which advertises itself as the original of Yonville l'Abbaye—Delphine Delamare's smart double curtains, yellow and black, were still talked about by her neighbors, like her blue-and-silver wallpaper. Today her house is gone (two different houses have competed for that title), her tombstone has been lost or stolen, but her garden is there, the property of the village pharmacist, who displays in his shop what purports to be Monsieur Homais' counter.

The real Monsieur Homais was probably legion. Flaubert is said to have spent a month at Forges-les-Eaux studying the local pharmacist, a red-hot anti-clerical and diehard republican, whom he had already spotted and banded, but he is also thought to have had his eye on other atheistical druggists, birds of the same feather, in the neighborhood.

In short, *Madame Bovary* revived and spread a scandal (a second suspected Rodolphe was uncovered at Neufchâtel-en-Bray) that had been a nine-days' wonder in the locality, and Flaubert was no doubt sick of the gossip and somewhat remorseful, like most authors, for what he had started, tired too maybe of hearing his mother tax him with what he had "done" to poor Delamare's memory. At the same time, as an author, he must have resented the cheapening efforts of real life to claim for itself material he had transmuted with such pain in his study; even in her name, "Delphine Delamare" sounds like a hack's alias for Emma Bovary.

The gossip was not silenced by his denials. Indeed, it proliferated, breeding on the novel itself—impossible to know how much elderly witnesses, interviewed in Ry forty years later, had had their memories refreshed by contact with the novel. Was the Delamares' elegant furniture really sold at auction to satisfy her creditors? And the unfortunate doctor's "two hundred rose stocks *de belle variété"?* What about the "mahogany Gothic prie-dieu embroidered in subdued blue and yellow gros point?" by Delphine Delamare? In 1890, on the word of one authority, it could be seen in Rouen, the cushion considerably faded. In 1905, the servant Felicité (her real name was Augustine), aged seventy-nine, was still talking to visitors about her mistress, differing stoutly with others who remembered her on the color of her hair. "No. Not blond. Chestnut." After *Madame Bovary,* figures in the Delamare story, real or fancied, must have spent their lives as marked men. The rumored "Rodolphe," a veritable Cain, was said to have emigrated to America, then come back and shot himself on a Parisian boulevard. If that happened to an actual country gentleman of the vicinity named Louis Campion (and there is no record of such a suicide), it cannot have been part of Flaubert's intention. And the gossip, as always, must have been wrong quite a bit of the time. Even given Flaubert's passion for documentation, he cannot have set out to make an exact copy of the village of Ry and its inhabitants. How well, in fact, he could have known it, except as the site of the Delamare drama, is a matter of doubt.

He must have passed through it, on his way from Rouen, and certainly the village, even now, shows correspondences with the décor of the novel, though, as in a dream, nothing is in quite its right place: the church, the cemetery, the market place, Monsieur Homais' pharmacy, the Lion d'Or. The "river" behind Madame Delamare's garden has shrunk to a feeble stream, more of a ditch or drain, really, and the real river runs past the village, not through it. But there are the outlying meadows, the poplars, the long single street, which is an extended *place* in the novel; "Rodolphe's château" is pointed out on a nearby road, and along the river there are many cow-crossings made of old planks reminiscent of the one Emma used, at the foot of her garden, going by the wet-nurse's house to meet her lover. In the courtyard of the Hôtel de Rouen, identified by a marker as the "Lion d'Or," a suggestible person can believe himself to be in the setting of *Madame Bovary*.

Human suggestibility, obviously, has magnified and multiplied correspondences in a way no doubt undreamed of by Flaubert. The fame of the novel caused dubious and even false claimants to be presented or present themselves as the genuine originals. A notary in the Oise named Louis Bottais (or Léon Bottet; there is some confusion) pretended to have served as the model for Léon; he was unmasked as an impostor. The progressive pharmacist at Ry, toward the end of the century, modeled *himself* on Monsieur Homais, who he insisted had been drawn from his father—as though this were reason for family pride.

The net has been cast wider. A second—or third—model for Emma has been found in the wife of Flaubert's friend the sculptor Pradier, who made the pretty ladies, Lille and Strasbourg, that sit on pedestals like halted patriotic floats on the Place de la Concorde. A "memoir" of this woman, written out in an illiterate script by her confidante, a carpenter's wife, had fallen into Flaubert's hands. Did he use it? Louise Pradier was good-looking, silly, extremely unfaithful to her husband, and up to her neck in debt. In the "memoir," where she is called "Ludovica," she is being driven to suicide by her debts and adulterous anxieties; her husband, like Charles Bovary, dies of the shock dealt him by the discovery of his wife's infidelities and the bills she had run up. In reality, Pradier long outlived his separation from Louise, and Louise herself, though she may have talked of it, never threw herself in the

Seine. She was living when *Madame Bovary* came out and she and her Bohemian friends may have been persuaded, whatever the truth was, that she had "sat for" Flaubert.

This endless conjecturing on the part of the public is the price paid by the realistic novelist for "writing about what he knows." With *Salammbô* and *The Temptation of Saint Anthony,* there was no occasion for Flaubert to issue denials. But *Madame Bovary* was fraught with embarrassment for its author, who foresaw, while still writing it, the offense he was going to give his neighbors by the heavy dosage of Norman "local color" he had put in. And as often happens, whatever he did to change, combine, disguise, invent, probably made matters worse, purely fictive episodes being taken as the literal truth.

There may also have been correspondences with reality invisible to ordinary provincial readers but suspiciously visible to his immediate family: "I know where you got *that!*" an author's relations cry, in amusement or reproach. Take the following, as a guess. Dr. Delamare studied under Flaubert's father, a well-known surgeon, at the Hôtel-Dieu in Rouen; whether he was a poor student or not is uncertain. In any case, being dead, he could not be hurt by the book. But there was someone else who conceivably could be: Flaubert's brother, Achille, also a doctor, highly regarded in local medical circles. He operated on their father; gangrene developed, and Dr. Flaubert died. It is thought that he may have had a diabetic condition, always dangerous for a surgical patient. In any case, the outcome was fatal. A little later, Flaubert's sister Caroline died of puerperal fever. Whether Achille was in attendance is not clear. But the two deaths, coming so close together, greatly affected Flaubert. In a letter, he described sitting up with Caroline's body while her husband and a priest snored. Just like Emma's wake. Flaubert remembered those snores. Did he remember the operation performed on his father when he wrote about Charles' operation on the club-

footed inn boy—the most villainous folly in the book? Or did
he fear that Achille remembered and would draw a parallel,
where none had been intended? A novelist is an elephant, but
an elephant who must claim to forget.*

On the one hand, Flaubert declared *he* was Emma. On the
other, he wrote to a lady: "There's nothing in *Madame Bovary* that's drawn from life. It's a *completely invented* story.
None of my own feelings or experiences are in it." So help
him God. Of course, he was fibbing, and contradicting himself as well. Like all novelists, he drew on his own experiences, and, more than most novelists, he was frightened by
the need to invent. When he came to do the ball at Vaubyessard, he lamented. "It's so long since I've been to a ball." If
memory failed, he documented himself, as he did for Emma's
school reading, going back over the children's stories he had
read as a little boy and the picture books he had colored. If
he had not had an experience the story required, he sought it
out. Before writing the chapter about the agricultural fair, he
went to one; he consulted his brother about club foot and, disappointed by the ignorance manifest in Achille's answers,
procured textbooks. There is hardly a page in the novel that
he had not "lived," and he constantly drew on his own feelings to render Emma's.

All novelists do this, but Flaubert went beyond the usual
call of duty. Madame Bovary was not Flaubert, certainly; yet
he became Madame Bovary and all the accessories to her
story, her lovers, her husband, her little greyhound, the corset
lace that hissed around her hips like a slithery grass snake as
she undressed in the hotel room in Rouen, the blinds of the
cab that hid her and Léon as they made love. In a letter he
made clear the state of mind in which he wrote. That day he

* This account of the sources of *Madame Bovary* has been revised,
thanks to criticism administered by Francis Steegmuller when the
essay first appeared. As far as the Delamares are concerned, my present documentation comes mainly from Géraud Venzac, *Au pays de
Madame Bovary.*

had been doing the scene of the horseback ride, when Rodolphe seduces Emma in the woods. "What a delicious thing writing is—not to be you any more but to move through the whole universe you're talking about. Take me today, for instance: I was man and woman, lover and mistress; I went riding in a forest on a fall afternoon beneath the yellow leaves, and I was the horses, the leaves, the wind, the words he and she spoke, and the red sun beating on their half-closed eyelids, which were already heavy with passion." It is hard to imagine another great novelist—Stendhal, Tolstoy, Jane Austen, Dickens, Dostoievsky, Balzac—who would conceive of the act of writing as a rapturous loss of identity. Poets have often expressed the wish for otherness, for fusion—to be their mistress' sparrow or her girdle or the breeze that caressed her temples and wantoned with her ribbons, but Flaubert was the first to realize this wish in prose, in the disguise of a realistic story. The climax of the horseback ride was, of course, a coupling, in which all of Nature joined in a gigantic, throbbing *partouze* while Flaubert's pen flew. He was writing a book, and yet from his account you would think he was *reading* one. "What a delicious thing reading is—not to be you any more but to flow through the whole universe you're reading about . . ." etc., etc.

Compare this, in fact, to the rapt exchange of platitudes between Léon and Emma on the night of their first meeting, at dinner at the Lion d'Or. " '. . . is there anything better, really, than sitting by the fire with a book while the wind beats on your window panes and the lamp is burning?' 'Isn't it so?' she said, fixing him with her large black eyes wide open. 'One forgets everything,' he continued. 'The hours go by. Without leaving your chair you stroll through imagined landscapes as if they were real, and your thoughts interweave with the story, lingering over details or leaping ahead with the plot. Your imagination confuses itself with the characters, and it seems as if it were your own heart beating inside their clothes.' 'How true! How true!' she said."

The threadbare magic carpet, evidently, is shared by author and reader, who are both escaping from the mean provincial life close at hand. Yet *Madame Bovary* is one of a series of novels—including *Don Quixote* and *Northanger Abbey*—that illustrate the evil effects of reading. *All* reading, in the case of *Madame Bovary,* not simply the reading of romances. The books Emma fed on were not pure trash, by any means; in the convent she had read Chateaubriand; as a girl on the farm, she read *Paul et Virginie.* The best sellers she liked were of varying quality: Eugène Sue, Balzac, George Sand, and Walter Scott. She tried to improve her mind with history and philosophy, starting one "deep" book after another and leaving them all unfinished. Reading was undermining her health, according to her mother-in-law, who thought the thing to do was to stop her subscription to the lending library in Rouen. It ought to be against the law, declared the old lady, for circulating libraries to supply people with novels and books against religion, that mock at priests in speeches taken from Voltaire. Flaubert is making fun of Madame Bovary, Senior, and yet he too felt that Emma's reading was unhealthy. And for the kind of reason her mother-in-law would give: books put ideas in Emma's head. It is characteristic of Flaubert that his own notions, in the mouths of his characters, are turned into desolate echoes—into clichés.

Léon too is addicted to books, as the passage cited shows. *He* prefers poetry. But it is not only the young people in *Madame Bovary* who are glamorized by the printed page. Monsieur Homais is another illustration of the evil effects of reading. He offers Emma the use of his library, which contains, as he says, "the best authors, Voltaire, Rousseau, Delille, Walter Scott, the *Echo des Feuilletons.*" These authors have addled his head with ideas. And Monsieur Homais' ideas are dangerous, literally so; not just in the sense Madame Bovary, Senior, meant. An idea invading Monsieur Homais' brain is responsible for Charles' operation on the deformed Hippolyte. Monsieur Homais had read an article on a new method for curing club foot and he was immediately eager that Charles should try it; in his druggist mind there was a typical confusion between humanitarian motives and a Chamber of Commerce zeal. The operation is guaranteed to put Yonville l'Abbaye on the map. He will write it up himself for a Rouen paper. As he tells Charles, "an article in the paper gets around. People talk about it. It ends by snowballing." This snowballing is precisely what is happening, with horrible consequences yet to come. Thanks to an article in the press, Hippolyte will lose his leg.

The diffusion of ideas in the innocent countryside is the plot of *Madame Bovary*. When the book ran serially, Flaubert's editors, who were extremely stupid, wanted to cut the club-foot episode: it was unpleasant, they said, and contributed nothing to the story. Flaubert insisted; he regarded it as essential to the book. As it is. This is the point where Monsieur Homais interlocks with Emma and her story; elsewhere he only talks and appears busy. True, Emma gets the arsenic from his "Capernaum"—a ridiculous name for his inner sanctum based on the transubstantiation controversy—but this is not really the druggist's fault. He is only an accessory. But when it comes to the operation Monsieur Homais is the creative genius; it is his hideous brain child, and Charles is his instrument. Up to the time of the operation, Monsieur Homais could appear as mere comic relief or prosaic contrast. But with the operation the affinity between apparent opposites— the romantic dreamer and the "man of science"—becomes clear. Monsieur Homais is not just Emma's foil; he is her alter ego.

For the first time, they see eye to eye; they are a team pulling together to persuade Charles to do the operation and for the same reason: a thirst for fame. And both, in their infatuation with a dream, have lost sight of the reality in front of them, which is Charles. He surrenders to the dazzling temptation they hold out to him. What is it, exactly? The temptation to be something other than what he is, a slow, cautious, uncertain practitioner who is terrified to set a simple fracture. Charles has got *nothing* out of books; he cannot even stay awake after dinner to peruse a medical text. He accepts his ignorance innocently as his lot in life and takes precautions to do as little harm as possible; his pathos as a doctor is that he is aware of being a potential hazard to his patients. Yet when Hippolyte's club foot is offered him, he falls, like Adam, urged on by the woman and the serpent. After the operation, Charles' limitations are made public, and the touching hope he had, of securing Emma's love by being different from what he is, is lost to both of them. This is the turning-point of the book. Emma has met resistance in Charles, the resistance of inert reality to her desire to make it over, as she can change the paper in her parlor. In furious disgust she resumes her relations with Rodolphe, and from then on her extravagances have an hysterical aim—revenge on Charles for his inability to be papered over.

Both Emma and Monsieur Homais regard themselves as confined to a sphere too small for their endowments—hers in sensibility, his in sense. Emma takes flight into the country, where the château is, into the town, with its shops and "culture." Monsieur Homais' solution is to inflate the village he lives in by his own self-importance and by judicious publicity. It must be remembered that if Emma is a reader, Monsieur Homais is not only a reader but a *writer*—the local correspondent of the *Fanal de Rouen*. That is, they represent the passive and the active side of the same vice. No local event has *happened* for Monsieur Homais till he has cast it into an epic fiction to be sent off to his paper; for Emma, less fertile, nothing happens in Yonville l'Abbaye by definition.

Emma surely felt that she had nothing in common with the grotesque pock-marked druggist in his velvet cap with the gold tassel; he was the antithesis of refinement. But Monsieur Homais was attracted to her and sensed a kindred spirit. He expressed this in his own way: "She's a woman of great parts who wouldn't be out of place in a sub-prefecture." Homais is a textbook case of the Art of Sinking in prose, and this is the comic side of his hobbled ambitions: he would like to be a modern Hippocrates, but he is a druggist—halfway between a cook and a doctor. He is bursting with recipes; he has a recipe for everything. At the same time, he would like to turn his laboratory, which is a kind of kitchen, into a consulting-room; he has been in trouble with the authorities for playing doctor—practicing medicine without a license.

Emma's voluptuous dreams in coarser form have tickled the druggist's thoughts. He takes a fatherly interest in Léon, his lodger, seeing the notary's clerk as a younger self and imagining on his behalf a wild student life in Paris, with actresses, masked balls, champagne, and possibly a love affair with a great lady of the Faubourg St. Germain. He is dreaming à la Emma, but aloud, and he lends his dream, as it were, with a show of philanthropy to Léon. This is double vicariousness. In practice, Monsieur Homais' dissipations are more thrifty. When he goes to Rouen for an outing, he insists that Léon accompany him to visit a certain Bridoux, an apothecary who has a remarkable dog that goes into convulsions at the sight of a snuffbox. The unwilling clerk is seduced by Monsieur Homais' excitement into witnessing this performance, which is evidently the pharmacist's equivalent for a visit to a house of ill fame; and Léon, having yielded like a voyeur to his curiosity, knows he is committing an infidelity to Emma, who is waiting impatiently in "their" hotel room for him. In fact, between Emma and Homais, there has always been a subtle rivalry for Léon, and this betrayal is the first sign that she is losing. Léon is turning into a bourgeois; soon he will give up the flute and poetry, get a promotion, and settle down. As Léon is swallowed by the middle class, Monsieur Homais emerges. By the end of the novel, he has published a book, taken up smoking, like an artist, and bought two Pompadour statuettes for his drawing-room.

Bridoux's dog is an evil portent for Emma; he has been heard before, offstage, at another critical juncture, when Emma falls ill of brain fever, having received the "fatal" note from Rodolphe in a basket of apricots. Homais, to whom love is unknown, blames the smell of the apricots and is reminded of Bridoux's dog, another allergic subject. For Yonville l'Abbaye grief and loss only release a spate of anecdotes; similar instances are recalled, to reduce whatever has happened to its lowest common denominator. This occurs on the very first night the Bovarys arrive in Yonville; Emma's little greyhound has jumped out of the coach coming from Tostes, and Lheureux, the draper, her nemesis-to-be, tries to console her with examples of lost and strayed dogs who found their masters after a lapse of years. Why, he has heard of one that came all the way back from Constantinople to Paris. And another that did fifty leagues as the crow flies and swam four rivers. And his own father had a poodle that jumped up on him one night on the street, after twelve years' absence. These wondrous animals, almost human, you might say, are a yipping chorus of welcome to Yonville l'Abbaye, where everything has a parallel that befell someone's cousin, and there is nothing new under the sun.

Emma's boredom and her recklessness distinguish her from Monsieur Homais, who is a coward and who creates boredom around him without suffering it himself. Yet Emma is tiresome too, at least to her lovers, and she would have been tiresome to Flaubert in real life, as he well knew, because her boredom is a silly copy of his own, and she is never more conventional and tedious than when she is decrying convention. She and Léon agree that membership in a circulating library is a necessity if you have to live in the provinces (he also has a music subscription), and they are both wholly dependent on this typical bourgeois institution. The lending library is a central metaphor of *Madame Bovary* because it is the inexhaustible source of *idées reçues*—borrowed ideas and stock sentiments which circulate tritely among the population.

But for Flaubert all ideas become trite as soon as somebody expresses them. This applies indifferently to good ideas and bad. He makes no distinction. For him, the lending library is an image of civilization itself. Ideas and feelings as well get more and more soiled and grubby, like library books, as they pass from hand to hand. The curé's greasy thumbprint on Christian doctrine is just as repulsive as Monsieur Homais' coffee stain on the philosophy of the Enlightenment. The pursuit of originality is as pathetic as Emma's decorating efforts. Similarly with the quality called sincerity. If it exists, it is inarticulate, pre-verbal, dumb as an ox or as the old peasant woman who is awarded a medal at the agricultural fair for fifty years of meritorious service. The speech of presentation annihilates fifty years of merit—a life—in a flash by turning it into *words*.

From his own point of view, this renders Flaubert's efforts in his study as unavailing as Emma's quest for a love that will live up to her solitary dreams. Words, like lovers, have the power of lying, and they also, like lovers, have a habit of repeating themselves, since language is finite. Flaubert's horror of repetition in writing (which has been converted into the dogma that you must never use the same word, above all the same adjective, twice on a page) reflects his horror of repetition in life. Involuntary repetition is banality. What remains doubtful, though, is whether banality is a property of life or a property of language or both. In Emma's eyes, it is life that is impoverished and reality that is banal, reality being symbolized for her by Charles. But Charles is not banal; Rodolphe and Léon are banal, and it is exactly their banality that attracts her.

Rodolphe is superior to Léon, in that his triteness is a calculation. An accomplished comedian, he is not disturbed, at the agricultural fair, by the drone of the voice awarding money prizes for animal flesh, manure, and flax, while he pours his passionate platitudes into Emma's fluttered ears. "Tell me, why have we known each other, we two? What chance has willed it?" His view of Emma is the same as the judge's view of a merino ram. She is flesh, with all its frailties, and he is putting her through her paces, noting her points. Yet Rodolphe is trite beyond his intention. He is wedded to a stock idea of himself as a sensual brute that prevents him from noticing that he actually cares for Emma. His recipes for seduction, like the pomade he uses on his hair, might have been made for him by a pharmacist's formula, and the fact that they work provides him with a ready-made disillusionment. Since he knows that "eternal love" is a cliché, he is prepared to break with Emma as a matter of course and he drops a manufactured tear on his letter of adieu, annoyed by a vague sensation that he does not recognize as grief. As for Léon, he is too cowardly to let himself see that his fine sentiments are platitudes; he deceives himself in the opposite way from Rodolphe: Rodolphe feels something and convinces himself that it is nothing, while Léon feels nothing and dares not acknowledge it, even in secrecy. His very sensuality is timid and short-lived; his clerkly nature passively takes Emma's dictation.

Emma does not see the difference. She is disappointed in both her lovers and in "love" itself. Her principal emotions are jealousy and possessiveness, which represent the strong, almost angry movement of her will. In other words, she is a very ordinary middle-class woman, with banal expectations of life and an urge to dominate her surroundings. Her character is only remarkable for an unusual deficiency of natural feeling. Emma is trite; what happens to her is trite. Her story does not hold a single surprise for the reader, who can say at every stage, "I felt it coming." Her end is inevitable, but not as a classic doom, which is perceived as inexorable only when it is complete. It is inevitable because it is ordinary. *Anyone* could have prophesied what would become of Emma—her mother-in-law, for instance. It did not need a Tiresias. If you compare her story with that of Anna Karenina, you are aware of the pathos of Emma's. Anna is never pathetic; she is tragic, and what happens to her, up to the very end, is always surprising, for real passions and moral strivings are at work, which have the power of "making it new." In this her story is distinct from an ordinary society scandal of the period. Nor could any ordinary society Cassandra have forecast Anna's fate. "He will get tired of her and leave her. You wait," they would have said, of Vronsky. He did not. But Rodolphe could have been counted on to drop Emma, and Léon to grow frightened of her and bored.

Where destiny is no more than average probability, it appears inescapable in a peculiarly depressing way. This is because any element in it can be replaced by a substitute without changing the outcome; *e.g.,* if Rodolphe had not materialized, Emma would have found someone else. But if Anna had not met Vronsky on the train, she might still be married to Karenin. Vronsky is *necessary,* while Rodolphe and Léon are interchangeable parts in a machine that is engaged in mass production of human fates. *Madame Bovary* is often called the first modern novel, and this is true, not because of any technical innovations Flaubert made (his counterpoint, his *style indirect libre*) but because it is the first novel to deal with what is now called mass culture. Emma did not have television, and Félicité did not read comic books in the kitchen, but the phenomenon of seepage from the "media" was already present in every Yonville l'Abbaye, and Flaubert was the first to note it.

Mass culture in *Madame Bovary* means the circulating library and the *Fanal de Rouen* and the cactus plants Léon and Emma tend at opposite windows, having read about them in a novel that has made cactuses all the rage. It means poor Charles' phrenological head—a thoughtful attention paid him by Léon—and the pious reading matter the curé gives Emma as a substitute for "bad" books. It means the neo-classic town hall, with its peristyle, and the tax collector at his lathe, an early form of do-it-yourself. One of the last visions Emma has of the world she is leaving is the tax collector in his garret pursuing his senseless hobby, turning out little wooden imitations of ivory curios, themselves no doubt imitations produced in series in the Orient for export. She has run to Binet's attic from the notary's dining-room, which has simulated-oak wallpaper, stained-glass insets in the windowpanes, a huge cactus, a "niche," and reproductions of Steuben's "Esmeralda" and Schopin's "Potiphar." Alas, it is like Emma to stop, in her last hours of life, to *envy* the notary. "That's the dining-room *I* ought to have," she says to herself. To her, this horrible room is the height of good taste, but the blunder does not just prove she had *bad* taste. If the notary had had reproductions of the "Sistine Madonna" and the "Mona Lisa," she would have been smitten with envy too. And she would have been right not to distinguish, for in the notary's interior any reproduction would have the same value, that of a trophy, like a stuffed stag's head. This is the achievement of mass-produced and mass-marketed culture.

In Emma's day, mass-produced culture had not yet reached the masses; it was still a bourgeois affair and mixed up, characteristically, with a notion of taste and discrimination—a notion that persists in advertising. Rodolphe in his château would be a perfect photographic model for whiskey or tobacco. Emma's "tragedy" from her own point of view is her lack of purchasing power, and a critical observer might say that the notary's dining-room simply spelled out the word "money" to her. Yet it is not as simple as that; if it were, Emma's head would be set straighter on her shoulders. What has happened to her and her spiritual sisters is that simulated-oak wallpaper has become itself a kind of money inexpressible in terms of its actual cost per roll. Worse, ideas and sentiments, like wallpaper, have become a kind of money too and they share with money the quality of abstractness, which allows them to be exchanged. It is their use as coins that has made them trite—worn and rubbed—and at the same time indistinguishable from each other except in terms of currency fluctuation. The banalities exchanged between Léon and Emma at their first meeting ("And what music do you prefer?" "Oh, German music, which makes you dream") are simply coins; money in the usual sense is not at issue here, since both these young people are poor; they are alluding, through those coins, to their inner riches.

The same with Rodolphe and Emma; the same with nearly the whole cast of characters. A meeting between strangers in *Madame Bovary* inevitably produces a golden shower of platitudes. This shower of platitudes is as mechanical as the droning action of the tax collector's lathe. It appears to be beyond human control; no one is responsible and no one can stop it. There is a terrible scene in the middle of the novel where Emma appeals to God, in the person of the curé, to put an end to the repetitive meaninglessness of her life. God is preoccupied and inattentive, and as she moves away from the church, she hears the village boys reciting their catechism. "What is a Christian?" "He who being baptized . . . baptized . . . baptized. . . ." The answer is lost in an echo that reverberates emptily through the village. Yet the question, although intoned by rote, is a genuine one—the fundamental question of the book—for a Christian means simply a soul here. It is Emma's demand—"What am I?"—coming back at her in ontological form, and there is no reply.

If this were all, *Madame Bovary* would be a nihilistic satire or howl of despair emanating from the novelist's study. But there *is* a sort of tongue-tied answer. That is Charles Bovary. Without Charles, Emma would be the moral void that her fatuous conversation and actions disclose. Charles, in a novelistic sense, is her redeemer. To her husband, she is sacred, and this profound and simple emotion is contagious.

He is stupid, a peasant, as she calls him, almost a devoted animal, clumsy, a dupe. His broad back looks to her like a platitude. He has small eyes; he snores. Until she reformed him, he used to wear a nightcap. Weeping beneath the phrenological head, he is nearly ridiculous. He is nearly ridiculous at the opera (she has taken him to hear *Lucia di Lammermoor*) when he complains that the music is keeping him from hearing the words. "I like to know where I am," he explains, though he, of all people, does not know where he is, in the worldly way of knowing what is going on under his nose. His next blunder, at the opera, is to spill a glass of orgeat down the back of a cotton spinner's wife. He has no imagination, Emma thinks, no "soul." When they find the green silk cigar case that must belong to the vicomte, on the way home from the ball at Vaubyessard, Charles' only reaction is to note that it contains two smokable cigars.

Yet this provincial, this philistine is the only real romantic in the novel—he and the boy Justin, Monsieur Homais' downtrodden apprentice, who dreams over Emma's fichus and underdrawers while Félicité irons in the kitchen. These two, the man and the boy, despised and rejected, are capable of "eternal love." Justin lets Emma have her death (the arsenic) because he cannot refuse her, just as Charles lets her have her every desire. The boy's passion drives him to books, instead of the other way around: Monsieur Homais catches him reading a book on "Married Love," with illustrations. Justin is only a child and he weeps like a child on Emma's grave. Charles is a man, a provider, and he has a true man's solicitude for the weaker creature. He sheds tears when he sees Emma eat her first bread and jam after her brain fever. This heavy, maladroit man is a person of the utmost delicacy of feeling. If he is easy to deceive, it is because his mind is pure. It never enters his head that Emma can be anything but good.

He first meets her in the kitchen of her father's farmhouse. He has been waked up at night to go set Farmer Rouault's leg, in a scene reminiscent of a genre painting: "Fetching the Doctor." A succession of genre scenes follows that evoke the Dutch masters of light—Vermeer and Pieter de Hooch: Emma making the bandage, pricking her fingers with the needle and putting them into her mouth to suck while the doctor watches; Emma in the kitchen sewing a white stocking, darting her tongue into a liqueur glass of curaçao; Emma in the farmyard under a silk parasol. In the big kitchen Charles' senses are heated as she cools her cheek against her palm and her palm against the great andirons, and his mind is buzzing, like the flies crawling up the empty cider glasses, as he looks at her bare shoulders with little drops of sweat on them. He is a man, and she is a young lady; his bewilderment and bewitchment arise from this fusion of the sensual and the sacred. For him, marriage with Emma is a sacrament, and the reader never sees him in the act of love with her, as though Charles, ever tactful, reverently drew the bed curtains.

Why did she marry him? Flaubert does not really say. "To get away from the farm" is not enough. Would she have married Monsieur Homais if he had come courting? There are a number of questions about Emma's inner life that Flaubert does not ask. But thanks to Charles, the answer does not matter, because to him the whole thing is a mystery, and like the mysteries of faith to be accepted with holy joy and not puzzled over. For Charles, Emma is a mystery from start to finish. The fact that she ministers to his comfort, prepares charming little dishes, takes care of his house and his patients' accounts, is part of the ineffable mystery of her sharing his bed. The reader is persuaded by Charles' unquestioning faith, to the point where Emma's little gewgaws—her watch charms, her monocle, her ivory workbox, the blue glass vases on her mantelpiece, her silver-gilt thimble—partake of her seductiveness. More than that, these acquisitions, seen through Charles' vision, do just what an advertiser would promise: they give Emma *value*. Thus Charles is not only Emma's dupe but also the dupe of commerce. And yet it works; the reader is convinced that Emma is somehow *better* than, say, Madame Homais—which is not true.

Through Charles, Emma acquires poetry. But he could not possibly put into words what she means to him, and if he could have articulated a thought on the subject, would have declared that *she* had brought poetry into his life. This is so. There was no poetry with his first wife, the widow. Emma's beauty, of course, is a fact of her nature, and Charles has responded to it with worship, which is what beauty—a mystery—deserves. This explains why Charles, though quite deceived by Emma's character, is not a fool; he has recognized something in her about which he *cannot* be deceived.

Charles, like Farmer Rouault, is dumbly rooted in the organic world, where things speak in a simple sign language. A turkey delivered to the doctor says "Thank you" every year for a cure, like a votive offering in church, and two horses in the stable say that business is doing well. Flaubert is not sentimental about the peasantry, yet he prefers Nature and those who live with her and come to resemble her—as old couples come to resemble each other—to the commercial people of the town and the vulgar aristocrats of the châteaus, toward whose condition the tradespeople are aspiring. The peasants still have the virtue of concreteness, and their association with the soil and its products guarantees that they are largely, so to speak, home-made. Emma brings her freshness from the cider-presses of the farm, which she hates.

The country people in general are at a kind of halfway

stage in the process of evolution from the animal kingdom to Monsieur Homais. The farm men who come to Emma's wedding are seen by the author as collections of strange, out-of-date clothes hung on frames of flesh and bones—tailcoats and shooting jackets and cutaways and stiff shirts, reeking of history and doubtless of camphor, that have been kept in the wardrobe all year round and issue forth only to go to weddings and funerals, as if by themselves. These grotesque animated garments, each with a strong personality, have as absurd a relation to their owners as the queer cap Charles wears on his first day at school. The new cap, which is like a recapitulation of the history of headgear, is an uncomfortable ill-fitting false self donned for a special occasion—Charles' introduction to civilization, learning, book culture. The country boy does not know what to do with the terrible cap, any more than how to give his full name, which he pronounces in a queer way, as though it too were extraneous to him, a humiliation that has been stuck to him and that he cannot get rid of, just as he cannot put the cap down. A name is a label. Witness the penmanship flourishes of Monsieur Homais' names for his children: Napoleon, Franklin, Athalie. . . .

Many novels begin with the hero's first day in school, and Charles is the hero of the book that, characteristically for him, bears someone else's name. *Madame Bovary* starts with his appearance among his jeering schoolfellows and ends with his death. Charles is docile. It does not occur to him to rebel. His mother, his teachers, his schoolmates, and finally the widow, make a citizen of him. They equip him with a profession, for which he is totally unfitted but which he wears, like the cap he has been given, mildly and without protest. He did not choose to be a doctor; he did not choose his name; he did not choose the widow. The only thing in life he chooses is Emma. She is his first and last piece of self-expression. Or not quite the last. When she is taken away from him, his reverence and gratitude to the universe turn to blasphemy. "I hate your God!" he bursts out to the curé, who is trying to console him with commonplaces. "Still the spirit of rebellion," the priest answers, with an ecclesiastical sigh.

Now at first glance this appears to be an irony, since Charles has never rebelled until that moment against anything, let alone God. But Flaubert's ironies are deceptive, and what sounds like an irony is often the simple truth, making a double irony. The priest is right. From the very beginning, Charles has been an obstinate example of passive resistance to the forces of the time and the milieu. A proof of this is that, in all his days, he pronounces only one platitude. His love for Emma is the deepest sign of that obstination. He loves her in the teeth of circumstance, opinion, prudent self-interest, in the teeth even of Emma herself.

This passive resistance of Charles', taking the form of a love of beauty, seems to come from nowhere. There is nothing in Charles' history to explain it: a drunken father, a dissatisfied mother, a poor education, broken off for lack of money. Add to this a very middling I.Q. No program for human improvement could be predicated on Charles' mute revolt against organized society. He is a sheer accident, nothing less than a placid miracle occurring among the notaries and tradesmen, the dyers and spinners of the textile city of Rouen, where he hankers, uncomplaining, for his country home, which was no arcadia either. He is a revelation, and at the same time his whole effort is to escape notice, to hide in his fleshly envelope like an animal in its burrow. Moreover, his goodness (for that is what it amounts to) has no practical utility and will leave no trace behind it. As a husband, he is a social handicap to Emma, and his mild deference probably contributes to her downfall; a harsher man might have curbed her extravagances, so that she would not have felt obliged to commit suicide. After his death his little girl is sent to work as a child-laborer in a cotton mill; he has not even been able to protect his young. His predecessor, a Pole (perhaps another romantic; he "decamped" to avoid his creditors), whose practice and house he moved into at least left behind the bower he constructed to drink beer in on summer evenings, which in Emma's day was shaded by clematis and climbing nasturtiums. But the only reminder of himself Charles leaves in Yonville l'Abbaye is Hippolyte's stump and two artificial legs, one for best—bought by Emma—and one for everyday. Was he drawn from life? A little of him, including his first wife, the widow, may have been borrowed from Eugène Delamare. There may be reminiscences of a schoolmate, especially the cap. All that can be said is that Charles Bovary, wherever he came from, dawning in a vision or patiently constructed out of treasured bits and pieces of reality, was cherished by his creator as a stubborn possibility that cannot be ruled out even from a pessimistic view of the march of events.

Spring, 1964

Crushing a Butterfly

THE best thing about the recent meeting at the Mutualité*
was the Young Communist student leaders wearing red arm
bands or bits of red silk ribbon, like happy novices in some
religious order at the annual Prize Day. Glowing with pleasure or pale with responsibility, these boy and girl schismatics
nurtured in the Party and now feeling its disapproval (expressed parentally by withdrawal of financial support)
showed extraordinary discipline, cheerfulness, and patience
in handling the crowds, mostly their contemporaries, though
there were elders of the movement present in the front "hon-
orary" rows. Two giant Christmas trees on either side of the
platform struck the festive, family note. The occasional boos
and hisses directed at the speakers were in the festal spirit—a
form of sardonic applause accorded the enemy for his courage or simply for his long-windedness. No speaker was pre-
vented from continuing. I do not think a meeting of this kind
would have been so orderly and good-natured in the United
States, though it is impossible, really, to imagine a parallel
there, since a meeting on the topic of "What Can Literature
Do?" would not have been attended by four thousand young

* A Left Bank hall used for political meetings, somewhat reminiscent
of the old Webster Hall in New York. The object of the meeting was
to raise money for *Clarté,* a magazine started by Communist students
which had had its funds cut off by the Party when it became too independent.

people, even if the fire laws would have allowed it in a hall the size of the Mutualité.

These Parisian students expected something from this panel. Not just words but a word—*"Le Verbe!"* an angry man shouted from the floor at the end of the meeting. *"On n'a pas parlé de la chose principale."* The speakers whispered to each other in bafflement. What did he mean—the Word in the first chapter of Genesis or language, discourse? Whatever *logos* the audience hoped for, they did not get it, and least of all from Jean-Paul Sartre, whose words they had come to hang on. *"Ce sont les écrivains réactionnaires de gauche,"* a tall boy explained to his companion as they walked into a café after the meeting had ended, at one-thirty in the morning. For the students, the meeting was a sell, though it more than accomplished its purpose—to raise funds for *Clarté*.

The question posed was not faced with any candor except by two speakers: the novelist Jorge Semprun, a member of the Communist Party sympathetic to the students, and Jean Ricardou, a delegate, roughly speaking, from the party of the *nouveau roman*. Semprun said, in essence, that what literature can do is tell the truth; this is its political and social function. He cited Solzhenitsyn's *A Day in the Life of Ivan Denisovich*. There could be no real de-Stalinization unless the truth were told and continued to be told about Soviet life by Soviet writers. He did not accept the excuse that Soviet writers in the Stalin period "did not know" what was going on in the concentration camps, any more than he accepted the excuse when it came from Germans who "had not known" about Auschwitz. This was a plain, blunt answer to the question and a bold one. To vow to tell the truth, whether pleasing to the authorities or to your readers, is genuine literary commitment. I myself do not know of any other kind. Moreover, it is not a twentieth-century discovery. It is at least as old as Socrates.

Ricardou's handling of the question had something So-

cratic about it too, including a certain mischievousness, which
he showed in sounding and tapping the ideas of Jean-Paul
Sartre. Briefly, Ricardou's answer was that what literature
can do is to interrogate the world by submitting it to the
test of language. Language, for the maker of fictions, is not a
vehicle for conveying messages to the public; it secretes, if
you will, a message or messages in its own structures. To
weigh literature in the balance with hunger is the old Art-for-
Art's-sake formula turned inside out. That is, Des Esseintes
might say "Art is more important than a child's dying from
hunger," while Sartre says "A child's dying from hunger is
more important than art." In either case, it is like saying:
Commit yourself; choose between pears and yellow. Language cannot be opposed in a scale of values to man, since
language *is* man. In a world without language, *i.e.,* without
literature, a child's dying from hunger could have no meaning. This required courage to say, not only intellectual courage but moral courage, before the massed audience of the
Mutualité.

The rest of the evening was a series of evasions, sometimes
executed with a witty sleight of hand, sometimes concealed in
platitudes, sometimes brazenly posturing. Yves Berger insisted that life was horrible and that literature could do nothing, *nothing,* but give the reader surcease in the form of a taste
of death. This took not courage but foolhardiness; he was
booed, and one had the impression that he wanted to be
booed, planned to be booed, offered his martyred face and
lachrymose voice to the audience in the personally selected
character of the scapegoat. Jean-Pierre Faye had some witty
remarks to make about a *nouveau roman* of the sixteenth
century and the *"roman"* of Hegel, but he finished in seman-
tic trifling. Simone de Beauvoir, sounding like a smiling,
sharp school principal, read an existentialist lesson mixed
with ordinary schoolteacher's bromides. Literature communi-
cates a "vision of life." It is a remedy for solitude. It allows

you to live in someone else's world. In one sense, she said, all writing was committed, whether the writer intended it or not, but there was passive commitment and active commitment. The bad, passive kind was when the writer shut himself up in his ivory tower. She did not really say what the good kind was. The audience applauded fervently, possibly because it was hearing familiar words.

Sartre gave an exhibition of dialectics. He was in good form when dealing with the mortuary remarks of Yves Berger and with the labyrinthine "freedom" Michel Butor claims to offer his readers. As usual in his writings, he had a surprise opening or gambit. The others had talked about the *writer;* he, more democratic, would talk about the *reader.* For the advocates of "pure" literature, the reader was only a means, the work of art being an end in itself. For Sartre, he explained, the reader was an end, since the aim of literature was communication. Furthermore, the Sartrian reader is not just an end or target; he is the author's better half, his collaborator. When the author pauses to seek the right word, he is putting himself in the position of the reader. Thus the reader is joint author, since the author is joint reader.

This, in my opinion, was clever demagogy, whose effect was to alert and flatter a mass of four thousand young readers who had not known, until then, that they too were creative. It is true that the author not only writes his work but reads it as he writes. However, the reader or listener in the author is not the same as the real reader—unfortunately. The reader in the author is the *ideal* reader, not the sum of future readers, many of whom will misunderstand the author's words, just as in several instances that night the audience misunderstood the words of Ricardou. Perhaps literary greatness consists in the power to force the reader to hear the text as it sounded in the author's ears, with all the inflections falling in the right place; this is evident in poetry where the play of rhythm and tonalities against meter makes it harder for the reader to read wrong. But this is the reverse of the reader's "liberty" as described by Sartre the other night. In fact, the greater the author, the more the reader is held in thrall; he is dominated and subjugated by the author. Hence such expressions as "A powerful writer," "I could not put it down," "I was enthralled," etc. More correctly, he is subjugated by the author's fictions; I agree with Ricardou. Besides, the author, when he looks for the right word, is not, in my experience, looking for the right coin to put into the slot, which will then ring a bell at the reader's end of the line; he is asking language to tell him what he intends to say. Even when he has found the word, *he* may not know; the *word* knows.

Even more disappointing was Sartre's sudden drop into the commonplace when he settled down to deal with the question proposed for the debate. The French existentialist vocabulary (this was noticeable with Simone de Beauvoir too) fails at just the point where existentialism claims superiority over other philosophies: in making a junction with life. What can literature do? Sartre replied with a vague truism: it can "make sense of his life" for the reader. All right, but how? Sartre did not say, just as Simone de Beauvoir did not say what committed literature was and how you were supposed to recognize it or be helped by it. She recognized a new work, she said at one point, by a tone in its voice. But this is the case with all literature. How does "committed literature" differ from the other kind unless it is a brand name for some special product that Sartre and Simone de Beauvoir were unwilling to identify? Why? This evasiveness was all the more peculiar in that she spoke with an air of nervous bravery and he with an air of dogmatic intransigence. As though they were facing lions. But *they* were the lions; the audience was roaring with them. At least at the beginning. When Sartre had finished, the clapping, for the first time, was feeble. Yet he could not have been hissed or booed, because he had not said anything to provoke a reaction.

Sartre in his role of shocker, of a "diabolical" intelligence, found himself in an uncomfortable situation. It was the others, the defenders of "pure" literature, who shocked and sometimes amused the youth—particularly Ricardou, with his mop of dark curling hair, round, simple face, and strange dark glasses. One of the charms of youth is that it is attracted to a minority, and Sartre knows that. You cannot be a minority and in the majority simultaneously, and this is the current dilemma of Sartre and Simone de Beauvoir throning in France. Moreover, to bait the *nouveau roman,* which is mainly a youth fashion, is not as easy as baiting the "bourgeois" of the Nobel Prize Committee. It is like rending black openwork stockings or crushing a butterfly.

Yet to treat the *nouveau roman* and its newest adepts—the young team of *Tel Quel*—with any degree of indulgence was impossible for Sartre and his life-companion, since, to speak plainly, "committed literature" is Aesopian language for literature enlisted in the service of the class struggle, and however much Sartre has edged away from the official Party line, he cannot go over to "formalism," the stock enemy still faithfully attacked at Communist-sponsored writers' congresses, along with U.S. imperialism, Peking, and whoever else is seen as the current adversary. The *nouveau roman* is a formalist deviation and its attraction for the young makes it particularly dangerous. There was a time when Sartre was interested by what he called the *anti-roman* (Nathalie Sarraute); he seemed to welcome the destruction of that old bourgeois structure, the novel, but he is now alarmed by the breakage, which "goes too far," imperiling other old structures. A declaration of the autonomy of language, like any declaration of independence from the masses, is seen by him as a counter-revolutionary act.

In fact the term "committed literature" is an antique, dating back to the post-war period and designating an alliance of certain writers with the then-Stalinist Party. It has no other meaning—as was demonstrated, if that was necessary, by the two speakers' reluctance to define it—and for the radical young that meaning has been drained of significance by the desacralization of the Party, following the Twentieth Congress, Hungary, the Moscow-Peking split. In any case, outside the Soviet Union, where a state literature, "socialist realism," had to meet rather strict norms of commitment to official policy, the slogan never had much connection with actual novels and poems. Unlike, say, surrealism, it did not denote a school or "way" of composition. A writer in the West was judged to be *"engagé"* by the number of manifestos and petitions he signed, the initiatives he took, the demonstrations he marched in. Those may be legitimate criteria to measure the activism of a citizen but they do not throw any light on what literature can do. Hence the shadow character of the debate at the Mutualité, where a practicing school of young writers with an overt body of aesthetic doctrine was opposed by elderly generalities of the kind usually found in the book pages of conservative magazines and newspapers. The students in schism with the Party had asked a serious question and got from those they had most counted on, Sartre and Simone de Beauvoir, a very dusty answer. That was maybe what the young man meant when he interpreted the evening for his girl friend: "Those are the reactionary writers of the Left."

March, 1965

Everybody's Childhood

THE OPOPONAX, just translated by Helen Weaver, looks like the result of an accidental discovery in the laboratory of the novel. The young Monique Wittig (she was twenty-nine when the book was published in France) may have been experimenting with the problem of the narrator in a fictional work: what we call or used to call the point of view. The Jamesian problem. Most Western novelists today accept as a matter of course the Jamesian solution. James's formula ("Dramatize, dramatize!") has meant the end of auctorial description, including the analysis of motives and behavior— "psychology." Everything must be mediated, as the French say. In practice, this tends to cut out Beauty and Wit. Nabokov, in many ways an old-fashioned dandy of the novel, has had the daring to keep both, using the device of a garrulous false "I"—Humbert Humbert, Professor Kinbote—and, in *Pale Fire,* making a pseudo-collage by gluing notes and commentary onto a 999-line poem, the outcome being a novel presented as an *objet trouvé*. But Nabokov is an eccentric.

The obligation we feel to dramatize or mediate (which seems to bind us like a social obligation and probably has something to do with the spread of democratic notions, no one wanting to claim omniscience) has made the novel a cumbersome affair. It has seemed to impose the ugly flashback, since the past, by present convention, can only exist in someone's memory—not objectively in history or in the author's private knowledge. If you want to tell what happened before, you have to have a character "reliving" it. Also, as if to make things harder, novels nowadays never seem to start at the beginning of the story and go on to the end but plunge *in medias res* (again the drama) and then move backward, through memory, till the character is finally abreast of his starting-point. Or you may have flashbacks within a flashback. These shifts, which we all resort to, present company included, are ugly no doubt because they are false to the nature of prose narrative, which can be pictured as a long string, and false too to the psychology of memory, which does not work the way novelists are pretending it does. Memory does not tell stories; people do.

In France, the *nouveau roman* is using the flashback too, though in a somewhat more arty way, borrowing from films, the zero point being reached by an amnesiac narrator. But there is one modern French novel that has got rid of the flashback without "regressing" to earlier modes. I am thinking of Nathalie Sarraute's *Les Fruits d'Or,* which tells the story of a hero—in this case a book—starting with the beginning and ending with the end. It is pure linear narration, and yet the author is absent; the reader gleans what is happening from a series of, as it were, *overheard* conversations. Being conversation, it suggests a disembodied theatre, but the fast-moving theatre of comedy—Molière. By perfection of form, concordance of means and ends, the book (in my opinion) became a classic the day it was published. Here the convention of the hidden author and the mystifications surrounding the point of view suddenly make sense. The theme of *Les Fruits d'Or* is a question of value: are those fruits gold or gilt? Do aesthetic values have a "real" existence or are they only a fluctuating currency, undergoing spirals of inflation and deflation according to the market? Not Was-I-in-Marienbad-last-year-or-did-I-only-think-I-was?—a pseudo-question that could be answered by a hotel register. In *Les Fruits d'Or,* the eponymous hero—the book—is absent, being only talked about, and the author, therefore, must be absent too, not just hidden, but frankly hiding, since the creator who has imagined the imaginary book is evidently the only person who could know whether it was good or bad or neither. If we could find the author, we would know too, but it is just that certainty that is forbidden by the very terms of the problem.

With Monique Wittig, something similar seems to have happened. A technical experiment, asking an epistemological question about the nature and limits of memory, has led to a genuine finding. At first sight, *The Opoponax* can be placed in a familiar category: the autobiographical novel of childhood. It starts at the beginning and ends at the end, going from the first day in primary school, where a little boy comes in asking who wants to see his penis, to a cold June day in a convent boarding-school, where the pupils are taken to the burial of a teacher—an *Ite missa est* to puberty. There are no flashbacks. It is all, you could say, a flashback, since the author is not recounting the story but reliving it sharply in memory. But she is reliving it as if it had happened to *somebody else,* which in fact is always the case. Catherine Legrand is not a fictional alias or transparent disguise for Monique Wittig: she is a conjecture about an earlier Monique Wittig. It is clear that between "me" remembering and my previous self, there is a separation, as in the Einsteinian field theory, so that if I write "I" for both, I am slurring over an unsettling reality. But how to state that uncertainty in narrative terms?

Monique Wittig's solution was to desubjectify Catherine Legrand to the limit of possibility, so that she would become a kind of *on dit,* a generally accepted rumor. If "I" is ruled out as the appropriate pronoun, "she" is not wholly exact either for an indeterminate being who is not the author any more and not, on the other hand, a fictional heroine. *The Opoponax* meets the difficulty by opening a cleavage in Catherine Legrand, between a "she" and an *"on"*—an indefinite pronoun.

Unfortunately, this word is not translatable into English, and the translator's "you" could hardly be more wrong most of the time. "You" is personal and familiar; it is the word you use when talking to yourself. "You ought to do that, Mary." True, I can write "the word you use," meaning you-and-I, reader. But I cannot write "You played baseball," if I mean all of us played baseball that day. *On* is impersonal, indefinite, abstract, neutral, guarded. It is myself and everybody in a given collective at a given time. *"On jouait au baseball."* It is also an unspecified somebody. Here is a real letter from a young boy in *classe de neige,* which reads exactly like *L'Opoponax. "On ne fait pas de ski aujourd'hui. On fait le calcul. On s'ennuie."* "There wasn't any skiing today. We did our arithmetic. It's boring here."

The short French sentences of *L'Opoponax* often sound like a glum Sunday letter written home to parents. Or like a laborious school essay—a requirement. Monique Wittig uses the present tense throughout (cf. the child's letter), which again has no English equivalent. The narrative present in English is used for what the manuals call "vividness," and it is probably more American than English. "I come into the room. I see this guy with a gun. He jumps me." But we do not use it habitually; the French do, partly because the *passé défini* is ugly: *"Nous affublâmes."* The translator's second mistake was to keep the narrative present. Her verbs, far from suggesting an unfixed, undated time—a letter headed simply "Sunday"—make events appear wildly jerky and speeded up, as in an early movie. A third peculiarity of the original is the absence of paragraphing or dots or adverbial phrases to denote the end of one time sequence and the beginning of another: these dissolves and juxtapositions without apparent logic correspond (though this may not have been intended) to the lack of punctuation and oddities of punctuation in a child's letter, where you may find a big round period eyeing you in the middle of a sentence. The reader, obliged to paragraph this almost uninterrupted march of sentences, becomes *more* aware than he would be normally of lacunae, breaks, shifts of subject, indicating often—though not always —fear, as in a dream. This comes through in the English version, except for the quotations from poetry, which are left in French—perhaps the only recourse—and put into italics.

The discovery made in *The Opoponax* is a new insight into childhood and the educative process. The indefinite pronoun proves to be a key that unlocks more doors than may have been expected on the first try. The *on* not only marks a neutral relation between author and material: it marks a neutral relation of the child to herself. Combined with the static present and the monotone of the run-on paragraphs, it reveals that to be a child is not at all a simple, spontaneous thing. To be a child is something one learns, as one learns the names of rivers or the kings of France. Childhood, for a child, is a sort of falseness, woodenness, stoniness, a lesson recited. Many children are aware of this—that is, aware of being children as a special, prosy condition: "We can't do that! We're *children!*" Playing children is a long boring game with occasional exciting moments. It is obvious that children imitate adults and other children: that is known as learning. But the full force of this has not been shown, at least in fiction or autobiography, until *The Opoponax*. A child is a little robot, and the bad child in a class, like the boy who wants to show his penis to the other children or the girl who pulls a white hair out of the teacher's bun, is a bad robot, while the others are good robots. The idea of children as little individuals is far from the realities of their experience. They are all copycats, by choice and necessity—witness their singsong voices, their insistence on *correcting* each other, particularly noticeable in girls.

Everybody's childhood is the same in its essentials. For a child, it is a story he is memorizing under his breath, beginning with his name. As if I were to write:

My name is Catherine Legrand. I have a little sister, Véronique Legrand. A big girl named Inès comes and takes me to school. Our teacher is Sister. She is Belgian. Belgian means that you say *septante-et-un* instead of *soixante-onze*. Untranslatable. Sister is married to God. Her husband is in Heaven. We can't see him because there are too many clouds.

This rote voice, like a phonograph recording, is the voice of the class: Robert Payen Guy Romain Alain Trévise Pascale Delaroche Françoise Pommier Catherine Legrand. A roll-call, a show of hands. It is the same on the playground at recreation period. Recreation is playing games, and a game is something you learn too. You watch what the others do and repeat it. You count who is there. In summer, the roll-call has different names: Vincent Parme Denise Parme Janine Parme Catherine Legrand Véronique Legrand. Those others are your cousins. Pierre-Marie Fromentin and Pascale Fromentin are your cousins too. Their father is Uncle. In the daytime you see the Evening Star. It is the one called the Shepherd's Lamp. When you go back to school, the stove in the classroom is different and Sister isn't there. The teacher is Mademoiselle. She has glasses with metal rims.

Children do not so much observe things as *study* them, with a view to retention. It is as if their lips were always moving silently as their eyes wander around field or classroom, taking notes. The commonplace that the great outdoors is Nature's classroom (cf. the *école buissonnière*) speaks more truth than poetry about the child's situation, as does the game named Follow-the-Leader.

Catherine Legrand repeats to herself what the teacher says about ghosts in the forest, tells over lists of trees, plants, and cereals and how to recognize them, definitions of streams, rivers, and torrents, the way Sister peels an orange in curls, words like "tangent" and "circumference," how to make elderberry ink, which Mademoiselle says is poison. In an interior exercise-book—"Catherine Legrand, Class 2b"—there are the colors she sees on her eyelids when she shuts her eyes in the sun, the little hairs the nib of her pen catches from the paper that make her letters whiskery, the smell of her teacher bending over her, the untied shoelace of a choirboy in church, the big girls making the little girls undress and play doctor with them, being sick. She puts in important things, like Robert Payen dying or the river flooding or finding a snake, and unimportant things, like Reine Dieu's beige socks, and she does not know how to show the difference, just as, when she draws a house, she does not know how to make it look deep or put people in the windows. She has guessed that there *is* a difference chiefly from the way grownups act—when she brings the snake to the table, for instance—but even by observing them carefully she is not yet able to copy grownups. She needs "perspective."

A child is troubled by the feebleness of his means, *i.e.,* by his state of inexpressiveness. He may not know how to draw a house, but he knows that the house he draws is not what he sees (when Teacher says it is "very good," she is not telling the truth). In the same way, even polite children get restless if they are forced to listen to one of *them* make up a fairy story: they can recognize that it is not the genuine article.

Anne Marie Losserand's story was very long. Mademoiselle smiled and nodded her head as she listened . . . Mademoiselle told Anne Marie Losserand that she could finish her story in class tomorrow that they must leave right away or they would not be home before dark.

Some readers have objected that *The Opoponax* is not true to *their* childhood, because it contains only discrete sensations—no thoughts or emotions. But first of all, these discrete sensations are the universal data of childhood. Second, it is doubtful that children think: they reason. Third, the emotions of early years are either indistinguishable from sensation (Proust's *madeleine*) or they are attached to an individual psychology whose character, beyond a crude outline, cannot be verified by a later self. Whether Catherine Legrand "loves" her parents is beside the point: it may be supposed that she does because *"on aime ses parents."* The study of her parents as individuals would produce portraits—a quite different genre and outside the powers of a child.

On the first day of school, Sister tells Catherine Legrand's mother that she should leave now and Catherine Legrand is glad because parents, she sees, do not belong in a classroom. The parents of Catherine Legrand file out of the book and are scarcely heard of again. Mothers and fathers have no place in a socialized unit ruled by an *on;* they are an embarrassment. Similarly, a "Catherine" would be a gross familiarity in the context: it is always "Catherine Legrand"—the name she answers to in roll-call and that will designate her when she marries, seeks employment, receives social security, dies. The primary-school child accepts this civil alias with the desk assigned to him; he learns by imitation not to be a "baby," *i.e.,* his parents' child. And the lesson is ingested: what most of us remember of our school years is not the feelings we mastered or hid but the behavior of pens, crayons, inkwells, putting on our overshoes.

Yet in adolescence, at secondary school, this begins to change, and a still sharper division takes place in the child. When Catherine Legrand goes as a day pupil to a convent boarding-school, emotion of an intense kind does figure, and its symbol is the opoponax, a magical plant yielding a fetid gum thought to cure infection: it is the same word as panacea. The name is also applied to a sweet-smelling plant used in perfume. In the novel, the opoponax is a creature, bird or animal, invoked as a powerful agent by Catherine Legrand, who loves the boarding-pupil Valerie Borge. The opoponax is of a proud and surly disposition, dangerous when crossed. He writes threatening letters in vermilion ink to Valerie Borge to make her pay attention to Catherine Legrand; he will be seen at dawn, he warns, sitting on the window-sill of the dormitory and he can cause fires and snarls in the hair. Everyone begins to speculate about who the opoponax can be. Valerie Borge guesses and puts an apologetic answer to his letters in the study-hall piano. She tells Catherine Legrand she loves her too, and their passion becomes a legend (though no one knows about it), like the odoriferous gum, fetid and sweet-smelling, like a cruel fabled bird, like the poetry in old French and Latin they have been studying in class—*lento me torquet amore.*

The opoponax is an incantation. His source is probably the herbarium Catherine Legrand is making, but from being a medicine he turns into a pain—the pain of love, for which a balm is sought. The identity of the opoponax is the reverse of a civil identity: in the first place, it is a secret. The opoponax is power and defiance. He may also be the love that dares not speak its name—a creature found in convent boarding-schools sitting on the window-sill at dawn. When Valerie Borge consents to love Catherine Legrand, who is now a boarder too, the opoponax, soothed, is no longer heard from: the panacea has been applied.

In the convent, the magical rote of poetry has been replacing the lists memorized in geography drill and nature study in primary school. Individualities among the girls are becoming more distinct, and yet sensation is becoming more blurred and dreamlike. Faces, figures, are beginning to "stand out." In primary school, the chief distinction for a classmate was to die or to have a little brother or sister die—a mysterious important thing that usually only grownups are allowed to do. First you were marked "Absent," then your mother or aunt came and said you were sick, then the class tiptoed in to look at you, laid out under a white net with a rosary and a crown of white roses on your head. In the kitchen, your mother would be stringing beans and crying.

Death, for a child, is a pure *on dit,* even when studied at close range, and the emotion of grief—one of the least contagious of human emotions—is embarrassing to watch. It is more interesting to think about dead people being put into holes in the ground—children are interested in holes. There are a great many funerals and viewings of corpses in *The Opoponax;* adults for some reason act as if death ought to be a lesson to children. Yet in the presence of death children are unable to "school" their features or to feel the required emotion; they look for a distraction.

The Opoponax ends as they (*"on"*) are putting old Mlle. Caylus into a hole in a village cemetery. The pupils, who have already been taken to view the body, have now been conveyed, by bus, to the remote mountain graveyard. Catherine Legrand notes that there are no names on the mounds in this cemetery and that the wooden crosses are awry and neglected. To her and Valerie Borge, death is still unreal. It is cold in the graveyard. Catherine Legrand is saying poetry to herself. The last words of the book, a valedictory, are a verse of Maurice Scève, the sixteenth-century erudite poet of the school of Lyons. The reader shivers, for Catherine Legrand is not thinking of Mlle. Caylus: she is thinking (though she may not yet know it) of Valerie Borge. *"Tant je l'aimais qu'en elle encore je vis."* "So much I loved her that still in her I live." The past tense (in French it is the imperfect) is spoken for the first time, among the derelict grave mounds and wet field poppies, together with the pronoun "I."

July, 1966

The Inventions
of I. Compton-Burnett

A COMPTON-BURNETT is a reliable make, as typical of British Isles workmanship as a tweed or Tiptree or an Agatha Christie. The styling does not change greatly from year to year; production is steady. The specifications for the current model (*A God and His Gifts,* 1963) are much the same as those for the original patent (*Pastors and Masters,* 1925). An earlier patent (*Dolores,* 1911) was allowed to lapse. The setting is standard: a large country house, capable of being converted into a school—with visiting days for parents. There are a great many stairs (hard on the help) and passages, suitable for eavesdropping. At the sound of a gong old and young, brothers and sisters, men and wives, masters and servants muster in the dining-room. Other points of assembly are the nursery, the kitchen, and the common room. The period is late Victorian; the subject is human nature, cut from the old block, ribbed in the Adam pattern of murder and incest. Felix Culpa, an androgyne bookworm, is in the schoolroom, curled up with a popular novel, the Book of Job. His sister, Maxima Culpa, is in the library; a sulphurous smell of will-burning proceeds from the grate.

Detection seems to be natural to the English novel; this is true even in Jane Austen, where a Wickham or a Frank Churchill is "found out." The traditional English novel, from Fielding on, deals in lost-and-found identities, concealment and discovery. Unlike the Continental novel (or the American), it is a kind of commodity with a warranty of unfailing reader-interest contained in the plot, which works like a factory mechanism—the mills of the gods. One of the mischievous originalities of Compton-Burnett is to have pursued this insular tendency to the extreme, making it her trademark. She produces Compton-Burnetts, as someone might produce ball bearings. (Dickens produced Dickenses, but Flaubert did not produce Flauberts.) Hence the uniformity of labeling in her titles and the open-stock patterns of her incidents and dialogue. The author, like all reliable old firms, is stressing the *sameness* of the formula: senior service. Her books have a magic ingredient—forgettability, which makes them just as good the second time. She has no imitators. The formula is a trade secret. When she consents to give interviews about her work, Compton-Burnett is cryptic, like an oracle or a hermit inventor.

This habit of secrecy (possibly an effect of the genteel tradition, which frowned on trade and manufacture and still more on their inner workings, felt to be *unmentionable,* like undergarments) has given rise, naturally, to legends about her life and her novels—legends which, in the case of her life, borrow from the plots of her novels, though she herself has complained that life does not have plots. As for her novels, criticism quite commonly turns them into a sort of hearsay or third-hand report, and you can read in the New York *Times Book Review*—or the French review *Critique*—that Compton-Burnett "refrains from"—"often omits"—physical description of her characters, when in fact one of the peculiarities of her work is the stiff, almost arthritic care with which physical appearance is *invariably* rendered: "She was a tall very pale woman of about sixty, who somehow gave the impression of being small and whose spareness of build was without the wiriness supposed to accompany it. She had wavy, grey hair, a long narrow chin . . ." etc. The insistence on getting a "likeness," as though with the aid of tracing-paper, suggests some naif realist: the Douanier Rousseau or Grandma Moses. The *Critique* authority adds that Compton-Burnett's characters rarely have a profession (doctors, lawyers, authors, clergymen, civil servants, schoolteachers?) and that she suppresses such "inessential details" as entrances and exits, when actually another peculiarity is her uncannily clear stage directions. The reader always knows, as if by ESP, exactly who has entered and left a room.

An English authority states that she observes a strict unity of place. But the scene shifts from house to house, from house to cottage or church, from a house to a school or schools, and vice versa. *A Family and a Fortune* even has a long and somewhat tremolo fugue, when Dudley flees into the snowy night and meets Miss Griffin, another homeless wanderer—an episode that slightly recalls the flight and last illness of old Stepan Trofimovitch, tended by the Gospel Woman, in *The Possessed*. To stage a Compton-Burnett faithfully would require a great many scene-shifters or a revolving stage.

There is something in her work that seems to encourage false generalizations about it. She has designed her books as curios, and the fate of a curio is to be ranged on a shelf. Though easy to read, she is a hard writer to grasp. Her books slip away from you, and the inclination, therefore, is to "place" them conveniently. Most criticism of her is replete with lists—of "good" characters and bad ones, flat characters and round ones, "likeable" persons and tyrants; her critics are prone to count, divide, and classify, not always accurately, to measure the ratio of dialogue to description on a page. This counting, these laborious measurements, as of an unknown object—a giant footprint or a flying saucer—denote critical bafflement. Doubtless by her own wish, she remains a phenomenon, an occurrence in the history of letters. It would appear to be hubris to try to guess her riddle.

Her work is strewn with big, amateurish-looking clues, like

planted evidence to mislead professional pryers in search of meanings, wider applications, influences. She has a fondness for naming her people after the English Poets (no resemblance intended; that is the point), and one of her old women is named Regan—by mistake; her father had thought that Regan was one of Shakespeare's heroines. The English Novelists too, like a private joke, keep nudging each other in these texts, while the anxious reader asks himself what is the point of allusions to Smollett, Maria Edgeworth, Jane Austen, Miss Mitford, Mrs. Gaskell, George Eliot, Dickens. Is he missing something important? Where is the connection with the story? Many clues lead to Shakespeare (King Lear and his daughters, for instance, in *A Father and His Fate*), and the reader is early put on the scent of Oedipus, the Jane Austen trail having grown cold. The "incest theme," already prominent in *Brothers and Sisters,* reappeared in *Darkness and Day,* as though to confirm suspicion. Did the quirky author, hidden like one of her characters in the folds of her narrative, hope to overhear critics fondly talking about Greek tragedy in Victorian dress and the "stichomythia" of her dialogue?

The incest theme is surely a red herring. The coupling between blood relations (or between people who imagine they are blood relations) is never anything but a twist of the plot. The author is capable of the fullest realism in her treatment of the passions, including the sexual ones, but when she shows incest, it is not a passion but an accident. She is strong on presenting temptation, but we never see a character being *tempted* to commit incest, as we do in the case of murder. Anyone who thinks that incest is the "subject" of Compton-Burnett has failed to see her real interests and the real idiosyncrasy of her mind.

Her books are not like other books; they are, as she might say, books apart. They do not "relate" to their material in the ordinary literary way, but crab-wise. The subject of any given

Compton-Burnett is simply a cluster of associations and word-plays, while the plot is usually made up of arithmetical puzzles and brain-twisters.

Take *Brothers and Sisters,* which is assumed to be about the "curse of incest," since the principal couple, Sophia Stace and her husband, are revealed to be brother and sister—half-brother and -sister. There are six pairs of brothers and sisters in the novel, one of which is married. And what is interesting to the author is not the "sin" but its mathematical permutations. A child of incest, as one of them remarks thoughtfully, has only one grandfather; this is viewed as a deprivation. The children of Sophia Stace, thanks to her insistence on marrying her own unsuspected half-brother, are underprivileged. Behind the incest is illegitimacy: Sophia's husband is her father's by-blow. This in turn opens up new incestuous combinations at a second remove. Sophia's husband's ancient mother appears in the village with her legitimate children, who become engaged to his children, that is, to their half-niece and -nephew, who are both each other's brothers and sisters and first cousins. What the children of these new unions would be to each other and to their parents and uncles and aunts could best be worked out as a problem in algebra. Relations multiply, as it were cancerously.

And now a new hidden fact emerges: Sophia has cancer. Sophia *is* cancer, the disease at the center of the novel, which contains three doctors, an unusual supply. Her will is a parasite on her family, like a choking organism. So the subject of the novel is Sophia's will. Her tyrannical will equals power, and power, a malignant disease, equals weakness, since the willful tyrant, who seeks to control the thoughts, acts, and feelings of others, has no control over his own. But the novel began with a will—the other kind, a testament. Sophia's father's will, whose disclosure she fears, is the impediment to her marriage; she sets her will against it, seeing his testament as a tyranny. All testatory wills in Compton-Burnett are in fact puns on the enslaving human will, which is plotting to survive death. A will, however, in the literal sense of a document, requires a death to implement it. There are four deaths in *Brothers and Sisters,* and Sophia, a beautiful woman, is a creeping death, like the shiny mistletoe, fastening on her family. She is afraid of death, and avoids speaking its name, just as she avoids self-knowledge, which would "kill" her. Yet all along, behind her back, her children have been calling her "Sophia"; when she is finally dying and powerless, they do it in her hearing. The naming of Sophia by her children proves to her, on her deathbed, that she is known, after all, brought down to the common level, in a word, finalized.

The child of incest has only one grandfather; in *Pastors and Masters,* a semblance of three manuscripts, where there is actually only one, is produced by theft and lying. The same with the pair of earrings in *Two Worlds and Their Ways,* which go their separate ways, crisscross, and seem at one point to be three. Duplicity is a moral case of doubling; many or most of Compton-Burnett's characters are two-faced. Coincidence, which plays such a part in these novels, is a sort of incest in the household economy of narrative: a single grandfather (a place or time or person) serves two families of events.

Events, in fact, run in families in Compton-Burnett's novels. The incidents in any given novel have a family resemblance to each other, and this family resemblance, which is often sportive, like the playful behavior of genes, constitutes the form. The novels are "held together," as a family is, by the accident of their birth—something, by the way, that is never revealed; we do not know the germ, the starting-point, of any of her works. The usual questions put to an author ("Do you begin with an idea or with something you have observed?" etc.) seem as out of place as if one asked God where he got the material for the world. In any case, the member incidents may have nothing in common, really, but a superficial, mocking resemblance, as a grandmother's eyes may crop up, punning, in a granddaughter who is otherwise quite unlike her. Or the likeness may go deeper, into the structure of the novel.

Take another example—*Manservant and Maidservant,* the best known of her works. The action opens with a smoking hearth in the dining-room. A jackdaw is lodged in the chimney, blocking the flue. What is the meaning of this? One of the characters is bold enough to ask.

"Why was it a jackdaw rather than any other bird?" said Emilia, bending her head with her slow smile.

Answer (not supplied in the text): a jackdaw, proverbially, is a loquacious, thieving bird, and we are just making the acquaintance of another loquacious, thieving "bird"—the young footman, George. The jackdaw is also a character in English literature. He figures in the *Ingoldsby Legends,* where he steals the Cardinal's ring and has a curse put on him; reformed, he is canonized under the name of Jim Crow.

George has been brought up in the workhouse, shades of Oliver Twist. His female opposite number, the young maidservant Miriam, has been brought up in an orphanage. The nursery upstairs might as well be an orphanage, to judge by the children's condition; ill-fed, cold, ragged scarecrows, they are ashamed to be seen in church among "normal" children. Their miserly father, Horace Lamb (one of the few books the children own is Lamb's *Tales from Shakespeare*), is too stingy to hire ordinary servants, so that his junior domestics and his children are all of a threadbare piece—charity cases. The cook is a religious fanatic, and the butler, Bullivant, a highly intelligent man whom Horace inherited from his father, is one of those accidents that happen in families; that is, he is a normal being, with no visible defects.

Meanwhile, in the nearby village, a solitary storekeeper, Miss Buchanan, hides her peculiar defect from everyone: she cannot read. This occupational handicap (not to say hazard; she also acts as a letter-drop) is tantamount to blindness. The Lamb children have a tutor whose mother, Mrs. Doubleday, has another form of blindness; because of her egoism, she cannot see what is going on around her: "Mother is blind to the result of following her instincts." Mrs. Doubleday is unaware of her handicap; she considers herself unusually percipient and fancies that she resembles George Eliot, whose portrait, in reproduction, hangs in her parlor, to call attention to the kinship—that George Eliot was a very homely woman has escaped her notice. Similarly, Horace, who is deaf to human misery, shouts at his household, "Are you deaf?" The Eye of God is invoked by Bullivant to make up for a deficiency in his actual knowledge: "There is One who sees."

The novel is also a parable: of the good servant and the bad servant. Possibly a parable of the talents as well; the miserly Horace buries his talent in the ground, like Miss Buchanan, who is hiding her light under a bushel. Or again a parable of the loving father and the unloving father, both characters being presented by Horace, who, like the jackdaw in the legend, undergoes a reform. So the subject is corrigibility: Horace is corrigible; George is incorrigible. This makes Horace (the lost Lamb) the prodigal father.

It is evident that Compton-Burnett builds with a rigid symmetry. Opposites are placed in pairs, as in a lesson. "Mother" is balanced by "Mater," the stepmother. When strict logic is observed, this leads to perspective puzzles, as in *The Present and the Past,* where the children have been taught to call their own mother "Mater," not to make a difference between them and her stepchildren. But when the older children's real mother returns, who is "Mother" and who is "Mater" to whom? Events are marshaled in columns, sometimes in contrasting pairs, sometimes in matching pairs. It is in fact a pitiful procession, like the animals going into the Ark or children being lined up, two by two, in graduated order—double file is always more gloomy than single file. A division according to sex runs down the middle of *Two Worlds and Their Ways:* girls' school, boys' school; girl cheats, boy cheats. But the book can also be divided in two, like the characters' feelings, by another stark principle: home, school. Or a third: old, young. The flat bisection is merciless as a ruler.

In lieu of toys, amusements, new clothes, Compton-Burnett's children have been furnished with hand-me-down maxims, mottoes, and tags—scraps of wisdom from the family ragbag.

"The child is father to the man."
"They also serve who only stand and wait."
"True generosity is in receiving, not giving."
"To know all is to forgive all."
"A poor thing but mine own."
"The golden mean."
"Where there's smoke, there's fire."
"A failure greater than success."
"No news is good news."
"There is more faith in honest doubt. . . ."
"To thine own self be true . . . thou canst not then be false to any man."

Such aphoristic sayings, by dint of hypnotized study, become enigmatic, turn upside down, inside out. When time hangs heavy, there is always that resource. You can shake them, stand them wrong side up, take the stuffing out of them, examine their insides. It is a pastime that does not pall, except occasionally on the reader, and is never outgrown. The adults in Compton-Burnett have got into the habit. They speak automatically in saws and proverbs, which they then begin to query. Polonius' maxim, especially, sticks in their collective mind, coming up in book after book, like a perpetual irritant. In these novels to be true to yourself (if there is such a thing) is—by and large—to be false to everyone else. The characters who are true to themselves prove to be villains, like the young miser Clement in *A Family and a Fortune* or the terrible murdering Anna in *Elders and Betters*. Only a villain would dare to be true to himself.

On examination, many other innocent commonplaces prove to be specious, particularly when they take a paradoxical form—a suspicious sign that a truth has been inverted. *E.g.,* the real fact is that true generosity lies in giving, that success is greater than failure, and that no news is bad news. Compton-Burnett's own work often has a paradoxical air, which is the result, however, of her empiricism: her interest in seeing how an idea or a verbal structure would behave if subjected to certain slight changes. Moreover, in the angular geometry of her mind forms imply their complements; a form of words prompts her to find its opposite and its converse, without prejudgment as to the outcome. The reversal of an accepted notion may result in a discovery. "To forgive, it is best to know as little as possible" seems almost self-evident in comparison with the original. On the other hand, a familiar maxim may hold an *unexpected* truth, which is the contrary of its common meaning.

"It is more blessed to give than to receive." "Ha ha, there is something in that," said Peter. "We have to have things before we can give them."

The maxims and apothegms are those that would be heard in an ordinary household and heard repeatedly. The penury of ideas, like material penury, encourages resourcefulness. In default of new ideas, the old ones have to serve. If sufficient thought is applied, their meanings can be made to multiply and act as queerly as numbers or converging lines. As someone says in *Pastors and Masters* of the plagiarized manuscript, "You wouldn't think one book would have to go so far." And in the same text: "What a lovely family group! An uncle and a nephew and a brother and a sister and an aunt and a husband and wife . . . all in four people!" In short, the old saws, looked into, become deep—fathomless conundrums.

Compton-Burnett's people, including the sympathetic ones, are more often than not sententious, prone to balanced utterance, quotations from Shakespeare and the Bible, which are questioned by the lighter and more rebellious spirits. Bullivant is a polished orator, and great promise is shown by the three-year-old Toby in *The Present and the Past,* when he conducts the mole's funeral service, copying what he has heard in church. To "talk like a book" in Compton-Burnett is not (contrary to what is said by some critics) a proof of inauthenticity. It is a gift.

Quotations and adages are the chief worldly provisions of Compton-Burnett's people and particularly valued by the lower orders, who have fewer of the other kind. It is this that gives her work a grim sadness, as well as monotony: the sense of a shipwrecked Band of Hope marooned on a desert island (England or the planet) with Bartlett's *Familiar Quotations*. Her people are survivors, battered floating bottles or time-capsules containing the remnants of human wisdom in aphoristic doses. "It is in the books," says a character in *A God and His Gifts*. "All human life is in them." As though this were not a credit to literature but a melancholy criticism of life.

The power of speech possessed by Compton-Burnett's servants is an eerie thing. Their voices, coming from near at hand, strike the ear with an effect of surprise, like talking animals in a fairy tale—the frog prince in the spring, or the horse's head hanging on the wall, or the speaking fish caught by the poor fisherman. Like those talking animals, the voices waiting at table have the faculty of omniscience, being given to warning and instruction. And the hands and bodies attached to them swiftly execute tasks, as in the fairy tales, beyond the power of ordinary mortals, *i.e.,* the leisured classes. These froggy, fishy attendants wear a menial livery, being bound by an enchantment, and when they remove it, on their day off, they are changed back into human beings.

Something of the kind is true of Compton-Burnett's children. Their treble contributions make you jump, like a sound coming from an improbable quarter. Audibility equals visibility in Compton-Burnett. Children who are not heard are not seen, just as a servant, waiting at table, usually remains invisible until his voice is raised. One by one, the characters at table materialize in a ghostly way, like lights turning on. Until they gave tongue, you did not know they were there; their place on the stage was dark. It is the *unexpectedness* of the voices that creates an effect bordering on the supernatural and reminds the reader of a sentient world all around him, listening, in the shadows. Children and servants are astral bodies.

By contrast, the family tyrant seldom surprises by his entrance into the conversation. He is already there. His voice is unnaturally loud; Cassius Clare in *The Present and the Past* seems to be equipped with a personal amplifying system. The family tyrant has the floor in perpetuity. Permanently wired for sound, he or she soliloquizes, surrounded by a silence. He harangues, accuses, complains. The questions he addresses to his household are mainly rhetorical—they seldom anticipate an answer, at least not the one they get. Or else they *enforce* an answer, with the dreadful command: "Say something! Are you dumb?" Dependents, whose lot is normally to be mute (that is why their slightest whisper has that mysterious audibility), when speech is briefly conferred on them are constrained to use it. Enforced speech is the monstrous brother of enforced silence. But since the tyrant cannot carry on a monologue indefinitely, he graciously delegates a small portion of his power of speech to his wife or his old father or some other privileged satellite, sometimes his butler, who are summoned up, out of silence and invisibility, to conduct a dialogue with him. He not only has the exclusive right to speech but the exclusive right to silence. He plays deaf when his wife is talking to him, if that is his mood. The refusal to hear is the supreme assertion of his power over discourse; it reduces the voice of his wife (or other dependent) to a meaningless noise.

In *Pastors and Masters,* there is a mute chorus of schoolboys. The same with the boarder-pupils of the Reverend Oscar Jekyll in *A House and Its Head.* We know they are there because of the speeches directed *at* them. Or a sudden rebuke, as was intended, like a powerful searchlight, brings a boy into view. But the very garments of the female ruler are audible: Agatha Calkin "rustles" as she moves toward her tea table in *Men and Wives*—a sound suggestive of the movement of a boa.

Speech is magical power in Compton-Burnett. The revenge of the speechless is underhanded by necessity. First, the murmured or muttered answer. "What is that, Tasamin?" "Nothing, Father." "Whispering, whispering, always whispering," complains a female tyrant. "Whispering!" a male tyrant exclaims, as if in agreement. "Whispering and questioning. The two unforgivable things!" Second, mimicry—the frightening gift of Aldom, the butler in *Two Worlds and Their Ways;* the impersonator steals or borrows a voice that does not belong to him. Third, eavesdropping. Servants and governesses listen at doors; children, who are small, behind sofas. There is even a case of someone eavesdropping on a *soliloquy.* The tyrant himself stoops to listen at doors and then reveals himself, striking terror. Listening, except when the tyrant does it, is another sort of theft—a pilferage of the family's private stores of information. It is tolerated in the butler and governess, because of seniority, and forbidden to the under-servants. After long experience, the family has to admit to itself that the butler, waiting by the sideboard, is not deaf. But an under-servant is forgetting his place if he exercises his normal faculties while he is in service. This is true in the kitchen too, where the cook and the butler alone have licensed access to the Word.

George, the jackdaw footman of *Manservant and Maidservant,* is a cautionary example of the dreadful fate of a servant who does not observe the rule of being deaf and dumb. He starts by answering a question—"Where were you born, George?"—with unseemly readiness, forgetting his place. Next, he is listening at doors. Next, stealing and defying his superiors. It is only a short step then to the primal crime—his master's murder (which, being less than his master, he fails to achieve). But the crime was already present in his wagging tongue.

George's master, Horace, has previously withstood an attempt on his life by his children, who, tongue-tied with him as usual, neglected to warn him that a bridge he planned to cross was unsafe. Their action spoke louder than words. Like George, his children had been wishing him dead; they had murdered him in effigy by melting a wax image of him, which they first stuck with pins, in the nursery grate. In this novel, as in a bad dream, the wish is father to the thought, which in turn is translated for all to read in the indelible speech of action.

Few thoughts remain hidden in Compton-Burnett. They betray their presence—this is the source of her humor. One of the charms of her characters is their transparency. You can follow what they are thinking as plainly as if they said it aloud, which often they dare not do. This is most striking in her hypocrites, who, true to their name, are always stage-performers. An amusing instance is the text for the day announced by Sir Godfrey Haslam (in *Men and Wives*) to his family assembled for morning prayers. "The eleventh chapter of Corinthians, the fourteenth verse." If the reader, pricked by curiosity, looks up chapter and verse (there are *two* Corinthians, a quiet joke within a joke), he finds: "Doth not even nature itself teach you, that, if a man have long hair, it is a shame unto him? But if a woman have long hair, it is a glory to her: for her hair is given her for a covering." Sir Godfrey, in innocent transparence, is preaching against his wife, using the words of the Apostle—she dominates him, and he is ashamed of it.

The unspoken thought comes alive in Compton-Burnett, so that you can almost hear it breathing. Something similar happens with figures of speech—metaphors. Whatever is figurative in these curious books is likely to become literal, as with Sophia's cancer or the blindness of Mrs. Doubleday, who illustrates her situation by being unable to read without spectacles. Even such an idle trope as "I can't put my hand on my glasses," fatefully calls forth a literal answer from the grave of the metaphor: "They are under your hand." "I had better put my pride in my pocket," declares Cassius Clare, absently feeling in his pocket. It is not only husbands and wives who return home after being supposed dead (*Parents and Children, A Father and His Fate*); many a dead metaphor is an Enoch Arden come back to life at an inopportune moment.

Words and phrases talk of their own volition. They are not simply the old family servants of those who use them. Take the word "patience," which (in *Pastors and Masters*) suddenly throws off its disguise and is found to be a "condensed form" of impatience. "Patience contains more impatience than anything else." As though the word had been listening until it could bear it no longer.

These procedures, strange in the novel, recall logical positivism and modern linguistic philosophy. Throughout her books, Compton-Burnett has been drawing the consequences from the entrails of habitual discourse. Her vocabulary is small—as has been pointed out, not so very much larger than the vocabulary of Basic English.

This is not an accident; the same reductive, puritan discipline is at work. She is teaching her vocabulary not to be idle. In the same way, she has boiled down narrative to a few basic plot elements not unlike the statements of symbolic logic. Her books never deal with individual destinies but with binomials *plotted* as if on a graph; that is why her people seem "all alike," although they are not. The logic of language, for her inescapable, works with the key principle of opposition, as stated in such simple pairs as *here, there; this, that; now, then; more, less.* Using these building blocks, what structure can be made? What can be *said* that has meaning? Compton-Burnett's people are striving to wring meaning out of language, where it must be if it is anywhere. Her books sometimes show an irritation with language and its propensity for abstraction, as though it were only *words.* Unlike Joyce, she does not care for nonsense, which to her ear would be simply non-sense. It is impossible to imagine her *coining* a word. The fewer the better.

Her characters seldom discuss general ideas. That is not in their line. Yet two ideas, which are perhaps only two insistent words, have followed her throughout her work: Nature and Equality.

"It is natural, is it not?"
"It is natural that you should remember it."
"It is the ordinary, natural thing."
"We cannot alter our natures."

There would be no point in counting how many times—in the thousands—the words "nature" and "natural" appear in her books and in how many different senses. Also how often they are implied without being named. A "natural" child, a child born out of wedlock, is an almost standard plot element; he is the cause of incest, since his parent will not recognize him— one touch of Nature, as the poet said, makes the whole world kin. And yet incest is "unnatural." Parents and children are unnatural in the other sense (unfeeling) and yet when they are most unnatural they are perhaps behaving naturally. "Give

me a natural child," says Cassius Clare; he thinks he means
an unprecocious one but he is really yearning for a slightly
backward child, a "natural" in the old sense. His wife gives
the word the sense Rousseau put on it. "It [a child] is a
natural thing. That is why it strikes civilized persons as
strange." To be "your natural selves" is supposed to be good.
Yet human nature is appealed to, in the customary way, to
excuse some personal frailty. "It doesn't do to make a tragedy
of these things. After all, they are natural." But "these
things" are what tragedy is made of. "Human nature writ
large" alludes to some sort of baseness; on the other hand, "I
think I am a natural sort of man," is said in a tone of complacency. "To be natural is known to be the rarest of all things,"
but "natural," "ordinary," "average" are often, it would
seem, synonymous. "Yes, yes, I am an ordinary man." "They
are as natural and ordinary as that." "I am just an ordinary
woman, with an ordinary woman's feelings."

Sometimes Nature is only another name for a sort of rough
equality in the human product. She is a factory who has made
us all pretty much alike at bottom; our natural impulses are
the same. Few Compton-Burnett characters claim to be different from other people though some are. When Sophia Stace
does it, the claim at once lowers her: "I sometimes find
myself marveling at the gulf between myself and the average
person." Or Mrs. Doubleday, seizing on the word "unique."
"I have heard the word applied to myself. Whether rightly or
wrongly, I am not the one to judge." She is blind, of course,
to the fact that she is a completely commonplace creature and
never more so than in her efforts to distinguish herself. Her
quandary is typical of the predicament of the majority: the
average person slightly objects to being average or, rather, to
being thought so; yet in his heart he is grateful to Nature for
having made him as he is. It can happen that an unusual person will pretend to be ordinary, as a disguise in life, and the
most evil of Compton-Burnett's creations, Anna Donne,

makes a point of being a plain, ordinary person, and the awful thing is, it appears in some way to be true.

Yet Nature has another side, which is the reverse of tame and ordinary. She has made everyone unequal, "one of a kind." She is responsible for freaks of Nature, anomalies of every sort, hereditary diseases, and abnormalities. Compton-Burnett's world is teeming with Nature's errors, and those who are most sensible of this are the homosexuals and lesbians, who do not mate in the normal, accepted way and cannot reproduce, at least when they couple in the way that is natural to *them*. In this world of paired opposites, they have no place; they are neither *here* nor *there*. They do not interlock; they are misfits, keys without a keyhole, two left-handed gloves. Not being the marrying kind, they are generally outside the plot, looking in with curiosity and sometimes with envy; what *they* do together can have no outcome but only repeat itself. In a similar position are the companions, tutors, nurses, and governesses, ill-favored by Nature in one way or another and attached, as solitaries, to the alien body of a family. Those who breed and those who do not constitute separate races. Genteel dependents and the staffs of schools belong to the non-breeders—sad mule teams under a muleteer.

Such deviate figures appear in all the novels, most overtly in the three that deal with schools: *Pastors and Masters, More Women than Men, Two Worlds and Their Ways*. But the question of abnormality is treated with the greatest force in *Elders and Betters*—the most fearsome and somber of Compton-Burnett's novels. Freakishly, it is the one that most resembles a "normal" novel, in that it meets a theme frontally. The events and characters are bound together in a dreadful unity. There is nothing sportive about their connection. Early in the book, a father and daughter are heard discussing the evolution of life and how lower forms reproduce by "pieces broken off themselves." This Darwinian overture gives the key. "Nature is known to be red in tooth and claw," their relation, the budding murderess, soon remarks, lightly. The theme in fact is the survival of the fittest—in the circumstances a chill mockery of the process of evolution, which here seems to be working backward toward the lower forms, who are better adapted for the struggle. Everyone in the book is a mutant—abnormal or anomalous.

It is a story of two related families, living in adjacent country houses, without other social resources—apparently there are no neighbors to call on them—of faintly Jewish appearance, although Jewish blood is not acknowledged by them, and bearing Biblical names. They are a tribe apart. The motherless Donnes have moved into this sparsely populated area to be near their relations, the Calderons. The youngest Donne boy is a cripple; they have a pair of peculiar lesbian servants, Cook and Ethel; the father has no feeling for his children or indeed for anyone but his sisters; his daughter, Anna, is almost a dwarf, with a head too large for her body, an irregular nose, and an odd, reddish tinge to her hair and eyebrows—the devil's coloring. Quite soon in the book, she expresses a wish for a standard latch that would open all gates and wonders that it has not been invented.

In the other, happier house is a chronic invalid, Aunt Sukey, who has an invalid's self-centeredness; she has been a beauty, which also puts her in a class by herself. There is an odd elfish young man, a spinster governess who comes by the day, with her orphan niece, and some original children who have set themselves apart by the practice of a private religion. The boy Julius is heard voicing a heartfelt prayer to his strange god in his Chinese temple in the garden: "Grant that I may grow up into an absolutely normal man."

Having observed his relations, the child is afraid for himself. Nearly everyone in the book is afraid, Aunt Sukey of death, Cook of a shriek in the night; in her unfamiliar bed, the housekeeper, Jenney, screams out in a nightmare; the children implore their god to protect them against the unknown—their cousins. Unlike the other books, this one has an aura, an atmosphere, created from the outset when a long-vacant house is opened. Though the father of the Calderon household is a scientific freethinker of the type of George Henry Lewes and has given his children Greek and Latin rather than Biblical names, he has not been able to banish the mold of superstition. Unlike the other books too, *Elders and Betters* is devoid of comedy, except of a spectral kind, while a good deal of the wit is simply an expression of animosity.

It is unique in another respect: the children's mother is afraid of doing wrong, the sole instance of this in the canon. Jessica Calderon is a completely unselfish person—the greatest anomaly of all.

Scrupulous, imaginative, good, and perpetually guilt-ridden, she is a born human sacrifice. By a monstrous reversal, she is driven to kill herself by her dwarfish niece, Anna, who persuades her that she is evil. The goodness of Jessica, which culminates in an almost supernatural penetration, is received by Anna with cowering fear, and this fear is not simulated; to Anna, goodness inevitably appears as evil since it is the opposite of herself.

To herself, Anna is fighting for survival, as though literally for her life, in a power struggle involving her Aunt Sukey's will. It is either her or her Aunt Jessica; there is not room for both. She cannot imagine co-existence (as well as between the sun and the moon!) and naturally she sees herself as a daylight, open person and her aunt as a dark force. Anna's will is stronger than Jessica's, for Jessica only wants to know the truth—something her niece cannot even understand.

But Jessica has already been marked for elimination, on the day there were thirteen at the luncheon table (or so it was thought, by a miscount). According to the superstition, the last to sit down in a party of thirteen is slated for death. Jessica watches her two families—brothers and sisters, parents and children—all jockeying not to be last, and is found quietly standing when the rest have taken their seats. Then she sits down. Her willingness to be an odd number (the oddest of all numbers, prime and one over a dozen) disqualifies her as *unequal* to the struggle.

The idea of equality—or inequality—is bound up with the idea of Nature, which seems to pronounce on both sides of the question. Originally social inequality was regarded as natural; this faith, however, has been shaken by the time of the novels, though no one in them knows exactly when or how.

"I wonder who began this treating of people as fellow-creatures," says a character in *Manservant and Maidservant*. "It is never a success."

"Once begun, it is a difficult thing to give up," another character answers.

"It seemed such an original idea," a third says, as if with a sigh.

"We can see how unnatural it is by what comes of it," the first retorts.

But, once introduced, the idea of equality does appear natural, not only as a "self-evident" proposition in political philosophy but by the very fact of having entered a number of minds. At the same time, social equality does not seem to square with the facts of life, some of which are the facts of Nature as well.

The discussion in *Manservant and Maidservant* has been provoked by George, the footman, who has just left the room. The equality with his master so ardently, even criminally desired by George is not a natural thing, and yet everyone, starting with George, feels that his desire for it is natural. For if it is not natural, where did it come from? He was not taught it in the workhouse; nor did he derive it from reading. George does not "know his place" and cannot be taught it by Bullivant, the butler, by Mrs. Selden, the cook, nor by bitter experience. The one thing George has learned in life is to know better than to "know his place." It does not advance him to know this; it does not make him a better footman, certainly—nor a better human being than Bullivant, who has found his place by knowing it. It just makes him different. A problem. The natural man in George is a criminal, in the same way that the natural child cropping up in Horace's offspring is a parricide. It is Horace's fault, of course, that his children wish to kill him, but it is not Horace's fault, really, that George grew up in the workhouse. Nor George's. It is Society's fault, but perhaps not altogether in the last analysis, since Society did not make him illegitimate; his parents did. George is a Jim Crow. A natural thing, like the jackdaw in the chimney (or the dead mouse brought in by Plautus, the cat, in *Mother and Son*), spreads consternation in civilized society, which does not know what to do with it—it is there but it does not "belong."

The question of equality is seen from another angle in the kitchen. "We cannot choose our walk in life," says Bullivant dryly, "and there would be many fewer if we could." The cook draws a different moral, excusing Miriam, the maidservant, for her unwillingness to share things. "It is the orphanage routine. Things would be communal beyond the natural point." The cook does not specify where the natural point would be. That is the mystery.

The omnipresence of servants in Compton-Burnett is a chronic reminder, like a cough, of the fact of inequality. Their function in the books is to testify that they are *there*. Like witnesses in the box in a murder trial, they bask in the unaccustomed limelight—they are having their day in court. One thing they will never do is to pretend to relish their employment. They are not just commentators but living comments. Being in service has not always brought out the best in them. Below stairs, in the nether regions of the servants' hall, there is a ceremonious class society presided over by the infernal butler and his queen and ally, the cook, who are at liberty there, when not summoned by a bell, to devil their subordinates and conduct an antiphonal dialogue, sonorous like prayers and responses, over their subordinates' heads. It is some compensation for being a servant that there are others still lower on the scale. But not enough—something the cynical George sees clearly and that explains his lack of incentive to better himself in his calling. A servant is a servant, as he reminds Bullivant.

The servants below stairs and the children above stairs are the weak in the social structure, which in the case of children is also the natural structure. It is natural that children should be weaker than their parents, and it seems to be natural too (at least it is taken for granted) that those who have the shortest legs should have the most stairs to climb. Like the servants, the children are the first to feel the pinch of economy. Saving begins above and below stairs, where it does not show. No one questions the principle that children and servants should have inferior food, just as no one questions the principle that food in boarding-schools should be wretched. Decent food, apparently, does not need to be "wasted" on people who are naturally hungry. The principle obtains in the kitchen too where the younger servants, who work the hardest, receive the scantiest rations.

The concern with "place"—*i.e.,* where you belong, as though it were a physical space—seems to require that no one should put himself in anyone else's, even in imagination. It is too risky. Except among children and the women who take care of them, fellow-feeling is extremely rare in Compton-Burnett's characters. Those who show it are generally those who have no place of their own. It is an unusual mother, for instance, who shows imaginative sympathy with her children.

A repeated humiliation the children undergo is to be made to wear old, out-of-fashion, pieced-out clothes for festive occasions. The "best dress" of a Compton-Burnett schoolgirl (like that of her schoolmistress), instead of being a covering, is a sort of nightmare nakedness—a public exposure of lack of means. Clothes are important in Compton-Burnett, though their exact cut and material (except Miss Munday's satin in *More Women than Men*) is left to the reader's horror-struck imagination. Far from being appearance, they are brute reality. You can lie, as a school pupil in uniform, about your home circumstances, but your best dress, when you are forced to put it on, tells the true story.

Death is a great test for the wardrobe. It is a proud moment when Mrs. Selden in reply to Bullivant's question ("And have you mourning of a suitable character happening to lie by you?") is able to announce: "I am in a position to appear in black from head to foot." The trappings of woe are a grandiose proclamation, not only of financial status but of moral superiority. Mourning, like a bridal veil, dignifies the wearer and constitutes a sort of promotion.

More Women than Men (which contains two practicing homosexuals and three practicing lesbians) is packed with clothes, mostly old. The only new ones are bought by the principals at weddings and funerals. The awful headmistress, Josephine, cannot resist a roguish allusion to "my sable form" when she appears among her teachers in the common room, conscious that her subordinates are still further humbled by the visible signs of her loss. Her husband, subtracted from her, has become an addition to her womanly charms. Her middle-aged coyness ("my experienced phiz," "[my] mature form," "my sable array") puts a bold front on what would normally be liabilities. Her wretched teachers are *betrayed* by their clothes, but Josephine is a successful liar, and her sable array is the best kind of lie—one that does not resort to verbalization.

Her grieving for her lost consort is pure parade. But in fact no one really feels death as he should. The one who is capable of doing so is, unfortunately, at that moment beyond feeling, *i.e.,* the deceased. We can never be quite as sorry for the death of someone else as we would be for our own—this proposition is bedrock in Compton-Burnett's thought. The dead man's tragedy is that he is not there to mourn himself, since no one else can do it as well for him. And yet, as long as he is alive, a man cannot feel his own approaching death as real or probable. Indeed, the nearer it approaches, the more he disbelieves. So he is unable to mourn his own loss in advance, attractive as the idea seems.

Nature, our unnatural mother, has arranged that we shall all die. But to any one man, his death is an unthinkable injustice, something that should not be done to *him*. That no one can share his feeling—at least with the same bitterness and sense of outrage—seems to prove that injustice is universally condoned. Proverbially, death makes us all equal, but we could not appreciate the equity of this unless we were all to die at the same time. That, however, would leave no mourners—another unthinkable thought. Between the living and the dead, there is a gross inequality, even though the dead, like the poor, are believed not to feel it. There is a "gulf." Death and life are a mismatched pair, the extreme example of incompatible opposites.

It is revealing that Anna (a blunt instrument) in *Elders and Betters* is able to speak of death as if it were an ordinary, everyday occurrence, which of course it is. She asks how her mother died, and when her father tells her that it was a chill that went to the lungs: " 'Well, what could be more ordinary than that?' said his daughter, rising and hastening to the door on some other concern." Looking back, the reader can see that this should have readied him for a murder. In the same book, the *abnormality* of death (for that is how it appears to a normal person) is keenly felt by the invalid Aunt Sukey, who has been given a short time to live. She cannot help noticing that no one in her family seems to want to know this. And it is true that they are embarrassed to admit that she may be dying, *i.e.,* that she is different.

In the opening scene of *The Present and the Past,* the children are playing near the hen coop. One hen is sick, and the others have begun to peck it—the One and the Many, the strong and the weak. The hen dies, but Toby, the three-year-old, does not understand finality. "Poor hen fall down. But soon be well again." "Hens don't mind dying," lies the nursery-governess. "They die too easily." The children are not totally convinced. "It was pecked when it was dying," one of the older boys objects. "They always do that, sir," says William, the gardener, with an air of offering comfort.

All Compton-Burnett's books are concerned with Nature, Equality, and Death. That is what they are "about." Nature is brought to the fore in *The Present and the Past.* In the ordinary sense of plants and animals. It is the only book where a gardener is found in the cast of characters; off stage, toward the end, there is a village flower show. Toby is strongly attached to William, who drinks beer. On the afternoon of the hen's death, William, whom Toby is "helping," finds a dead mole. "Well, everything dies in the end, miss," he says to Toby's sister, Megan. "It will happen to us all." Being close to Nature, he is on easy terms with death. Megan's face clears "at the thought of this common fate." Because she is young, with a child's fair-mindedness, equality makes it "all right."

Equality does not make it all right with the children's father, Cassius. He aims to be superior to the mole. A self-pitying man, he hankers to commit suicide in order to be the center of attention and to make his family sorry they have not loved him more. What deters him is that he would not be there to witness the general grief. Cassius' dilemma is a ridiculous *précis* of the dilemma of anyone confronting his own extinction. Cassius proposes to eat his cake and have it. By simulating suicide, he provides for his own death and resurrection. It works, but there is a sequel. His family discovers the trick. Shortly afterward, he has a heart attack and goes into a coma; his butler, feeling that he is shamming again, does not call a doctor. Cassius dies, and everyone *is* sorry, but he is not there to see it.

Among Cassius' other errors is the fatal notion that he can have two wives at once, his ex-wife and his present one. He also errs in treating his butler as a second self, which gives the butler, who is a humbug like Cassius, the false idea that he is a sort of junior brother to his master. This is a contributory cause of Cassius' death, since Ainger, his vanity swollen by Cassius' confidences, takes it on himself to decide whether a doctor should be called: Cassius' wife is absent, and his old father yields to the butler's judgment that Cassius should be taught a lesson. His suicide was meant to be a lesson to his family (like Hetta Ponsonby's disappearing act in *Daughters and Sons*), the motto being that if you try to teach a lesson, you may learn one. In a sense, after all, Cassius dies by his own hand; his false suicide contained a real death inside it, like a loaded cartridge, and his sole achievement is to manage to kill himself while being too cowardly to take his own life.

The past and the present are evidently opposites—in language mutually exclusive, in life not always. Unlike a dead person, the past *can* rise again and mortify the present—which may simply prove, though, that "past" was a misnomer. The present can try to bury the past, an operation that is most atrocious when it is most successful. The substitution of a stepmother for a dead mother is an odious instance. It leads the stunned children to ask whether a dead person can be *replaced*—a shocking question to an innocent mind. Adults evade it. To the children, their real mother is both absent and present, present in the shape of a blank, where her place was. Missing someone in Compton-Burnett is always conceived spatially. When the space is filled by a new wife, is it the same space or is it altered by what fills it? If it is altered, what happens to the original space? Where is it?

There is no room for the dead in practical life or for the

past either. That is why people try to suppress it. Yet the past, even when it consents to die, has a feeble sort of immortality owing to its persistence in memory, just as the idea of equality cannot be laid to rest once it has been thought of. This defective and inadequate immortality is a property of mind. It is attached most vigorously, by common consent, to works of art. Hence the books and authors in Compton-Burnett.

She is wryly, uncomfortably aware of belonging to a long-lived species, the family of authors, whom she looks on with that mixture of tolerance, dislike, hilarity, affection, embarrassment that makes up family feeling. Here, surely, is the reason the names of authors are fastened, so inappropriately, almost unkindly, on her characters (Dr. Chaucer and his niece, Miss Bunyan), as children are named for great-aunts and grandparents without being given any choice in the matter. She is not especially proud of her family tree; many of the old writers were not nice people, and they all profited from the advantage they had over ordinary men and women. Ordinary men and women "live on" in their descendants—a biological fancy that is not especially consoling. But authors have a double life and, in principle, a double chance of survival, through their brain-children, who will certainly outlive them (that is the vexing part) and may attain a fabulous age.

The poetical extracts sprinkled through her work are testimonials to this longevity. In *Darkness and Day,* the servants are ruminating in the servants' hall. " 'To thine own self be true.' " "Who said the words?" a voice demands, and another voice issues, as if from a cave: "Deep things become dispersed." In other words, the corpus of Shakespeare has been acting like a corpse—slowly decomposing and enriching the humus. His name may be lost, but the ashes of his work have been scattered abroad. Or, having rained down, he has been returned to Heaven in the form of a cloud, whence he redescends, repeating the process *ad infinitum.*

Being an immortal, the author is manifestly a god, just as God is an immortal fictional character (perhaps Compton-Burnett's favorite villain) described in the Good Book. Such an author, Hereward Egerton, is the epic hero of her latest novel, *A God and His Gifts.* He is named after Hereward the Wake—an allusion to Charles Kingsley's novel and to an early literary forgery. The "creative" writer has figured in a minor way in many of the novels, but he has usually been a failed writer or a failing one, like John Ponsonby in *Daughters and Sons.* Here he expands into a cosmic joke, filling the whole sky.

Hereward Egerton, a popular novelist, is a household word. His fertile imagination has brought happiness to the multitude. He breeds best sellers and the other kind of progeny, as is fitting for a "genius," begetting them on his wife, his wife's sister, his son's fiancée. He is "at work" on the fiancée of a second son when his course is finally arrested. The names of the fiancées are italicized in the text, like titles. " 'Her name is *Beatrice,* and she is called *Trissie.*' " His amorous history somewhat recalls Dickens'; Dickens had a popular magazine which he called *Household Words.*

Owing to his copious royalties, Hereward descends in a shower of gold on the Danaës of his household. The mystery of capital, which has the power of breeding when invested, is much discussed by his old parents, whom he supports. Hereward is the family capital, the goose that lays the golden eggs; he is a talented fool, who, his father feels, is practicing a womanish profession that unaccountably *pays.* Like capital, Hereward's tendency is monopolistic. As he says to his son Merton, who is trying to be a "serious" writer: "One writer in a house is enough."

One breeder in a house would be enough too, if Hereward were left to follow his natural inclinations. Like all full-grown males still at the breeding age in Compton-Burnett, he resents having younger full-grown males under his roof. By his own unaided efforts, his family is multiplying. His Jovian relation with his sister stops just short of incest; he has found a better use for her, as the partner of his toil.

Power over the word, which Hereward enjoys *ex cathedra* as head of the family, has been extended to power over words, which makes him "a law unto himself," the usual claim of authors. Vicariously, through his books, he has entered thousands of homes. It is this that gives him licensed access to all the females in his family. He feels himself as all-pervasive, like light. The young women he impregnates are his public—admiring readers, in short, pushovers. When he was young, he wrote for the few (and had a single, unproductive mistress), but now, in his maturity, he writes for the many. Godlike, he expects gratitude for the gifts he brings, the "seed" he has sown. He does not get enough to suit him. Like most domestic tyrants in Compton-Burnett, he has a sense of martyrdom—which he shares, of course, with the Christian God, who made himself the archetypal Martyr. No human return could be adequate to Hereward's thirst for appreciation.

Hereward's promiscuity has its literary side. The chief fault of the creative species is its indebtedness to life. Hereward is no exception; he borrows his material from the life around him—even, it is indicated, from the characters and events of his most intimate experience. As always, this indiscriminate practice is frowned on by those he "uses." From Hereward's point of view, his little loans are amply repaid by the debt society owes him as a creator. The relation between life and literature—a final antinomy—is one of mutual plagiarism.

In this ultimate volume, the literary theme, like a wonderful sponge, has absorbed all the others: Death, Incest, Illegitimacy, Nature, Inequality. The literary theme was present at the outset in the multiplying manuscript of *Pastors and Masters,* which turned out to be an exhumed piece of juvenilia and a miserable plagiarized copy. The obvious reason for plagiarism is a desire to shine plus a deficiency of talent. There is not enough talent to go around, though everybody secretly feels he could be a writer if he tried. Or that his life, "written up," would make a book. A natural wish has met with an unjust distribution of goods. The result, as in George's case, is crime.

Plagiarism—petty literary theft—is a crime peculiar to the educated classes; a number of Compton-Burnett's characters yield to its temptation: the don and the schoolmaster in *Pastors and Masters* (one of whom is stealing from himself); the children who copy in *Two Worlds and Their Ways;* Megan, in *The Present and the Past,* who copies a poem for the mole's epitaph and offers it as her own; Dominic Spong, who copies his own grief-stricken letter announcing his widowerhood and sends it to all his female correspondents. Plagiarism in reverse, as befits the bottom of the heap, is practiced by the uneducated young nursemaid Mullet (*Parents and Children*), who tells the children nightly "chapters" from her life-story— a made-up tale transparently "inspired" by cheap literature. In Mullet's case, the deficiency is not in talent but in the *un*inspired poverty of her real history, which drives her to invent. A respectable kind of plagiarism is the scholarly biography, described by Charity Marcon (*Daughters and Sons*), herself a biographer, as made in the British Museum from material lifted from other books and mixed together. "Books are very like plants . . . they come up out of each other and are all the same." Hereward is too "big" for these minor forms of plagiarism; he lifts his material wholesale directly from life and even though detected is compensated by royalties.

One of the excuses Hereward gives himself for his domestic misconduct is the excuse of social utility: he has lived to "serve" the many. He also sees himself as an "instrument," a sort of Aeolian harp. The idea of social service combined with large profits is a typical capitalist notion; Hereward regards his "investment" of himself in his work as a meritorious act which rightly pays dividends—exactly the attitude of the "creative" businessman, which is what Hereward really is.

It is said (sometimes as a compliment) that Compton-Burnett has no interest in social problems. The world she has made, because there are no factories or slums in it, is mistaken for Jane Austen's "little bit of ivory." But the poor in Compton-Burnett are, precisely, made conspicuous by their absence—to be inferred by the reader, if he is paying the slightest attention, from the horrible scarves, shirts, and petticoats charitably knitted and sewn for them by the idle classes. The toiling, spinning masses are invisible and unheard, like the silent chorus of schoolboys whose marmalade is being watered. Remarks are made *about* them, and the worst are the "feeling" ones: "We should remember the less fortunate people when we are in want of nothing ourselves." Compton-Burnett has as much belief in philanthropy as Karl Marx himself. Whatever her voting habits, in her writing she is a strict economic realist with no partiality for the well-to-do. Her writing is extraordinary in its lack of social snobbery. Here she is far ahead of Jane Austen and of most of her own contemporaries. She does not even have an interest in social climbers, a sure sign of secret snobbery in an artist. That is probably why her books, despite the swarms of servants in them, have not found a larger public. They evoke "a vanished world" of privilege too unsparingly. Nor can a liberal reader flatter himself that the disappearance of a servant class has lent these novels a "documentary" interest; conditions have changed, but the condition has not.

What flashes out of her work is a spirited, unpardoning sense of injustice, which becomes even sharper in her later books. In her own eccentric way, Compton-Burnett is a radical thinker, one of the rare modern heretics. It is the eccentricity that has diverted attention from the fact that these small uniform volumes are subversive packets. If their contents had to be reduced still further, boiled down to a single word capable of yielding a diversity of meanings, the word might be "necessity." From strict to dire. From "constraint or compulsion having its basis in the natural constitution of things" to "the condition of being in difficulties or straits, esp. through lack of means; want; poverty." Not omitting its uses in phrases and proverbs or "a bond or tie *between* persons, *Obs. rare*." It is a deep word, like her works.

November, 1966

More on
Compton-Burnett

Ivy COMPTON-BURNETT, now in her eighties, is the author of seventeen novels that are supposed to be as alike as peas in a pod. *A Family and a Fortune,* the seventh in the series, originally published in 1939, is the first to appear in Germany.* It is not the one I should have chosen, though like many of her books it deals with a family and an inheritance. Classically in Compton-Burnett, the money in a family is held within four walls, passing from father to daughter or resident aunt to niece, just as her characters are prone to commit incest or what they think is incest until matters are cleared up. Here there is a slight and interesting variation. The inheritance comes from outside, a pure windfall, which enables the author to show a power structure (the family) and how relations within it are modified by the introduction of a certain quantity of fresh money, neither too large nor too small, as in a controlled scientific experiment. Too small a quantity would effect no significant changes, and too large a quantity would blow up the cell being studied.

Two inseparable brothers, Edgar and Dudley Gaveston, have passed their lives together in an English country house. The time is 1901. Dudley, the unmarried brother, is attached in parasitic fashion to the married Edgar and his house and children. The two brothers are often seen walking on the

* A review written for *Der Spiegel* of the German edition of *A Family and a Fortune.*

145

garden path, arm in arm—a picture that commands sentimental approval from the family watching at the window, although the closeness of the relation, as of oak and embracing ivy, might appear to a dryer eye rather suspect. Edgar, whose children are mostly grown-up, has long ceased to be a conjugal husband to Blanche, who is older than he (all the men in this novel are married to women older than themselves, as though illustrating the folkways of some queer little pocket of civilization), and his entire affection is given to Dudley. The model brothers are in fact an abnormality—one person, as it were, with two dissimilar faces, a sort of voltaic couple. The relation, which looks parasitic, may be a symbiosis. Each is the other's second self or "better half." There is much play in the book on the idea of everyone's having a second self, the primary self being hidden from view. The second self, as in the expression "It has become second nature to me," is the public one we practice until we have made it, as we hope, perfect.

Symmetry rules like Nemesis in Ivy Compton-Burnett. As the novel opens, Blanche's relations—her old father and unmarried sister with a dependent female companion—are attaching themselves to the family as a parallel parasitic growth. Having lost most of their money, they have written to ask if they can rent the "lodge," a small house on the property. Unlike Dudley, who has "grown into" the family, the new arrivals require readjustments of the host body. The Gavestons feel it as a sacrifice that they must give their in-laws the lodge at a lower rental than would have been asked from a stranger. And they will have to redecorate suitably, lend their carriage, set extra places at table several times a week; in short, there will be a hundred calls on their generosity. But, as soon becomes evident, what is generosity to the giver is a sharp disappointment to the receiver. This "law" of human nature is demonstrable. The receiver is always imagining how much *more* his benefactor could have done, had he been willing, and the benefactor is always reminding himself of how much *less* he could have done, if he had been someone else. Neither is able to see the other's point of view, to get the other's "angle," which is literally a question of place: big house–little house, rich man's mansion–poor man's cottage. The lodge shrinks and expands, according to who is looking at it (to Blanche, naturally, it is "a good size," while to her father it is a "hutch"), just as a rich man's money multiplies in the fancy of others and contracts to a bare sufficiency in his own. The points of view, in human geometry, will never meet, even if the poor relation turns into the rich relation. Only the people will change places. That is what happens in *A Family and a Fortune*.

Uncle Dudley, overnight, inherits a small fortune from a forgotten godfather and at once, as he himself notices, he acquires a new psychology, that of a rich man. Exaggerated reports of the size of his inheritance make him start to feel poor in comparison, and to his shame he finds himself weighing the claims of others on his generosity. What shall he do with the money—he, a bachelor in his fifties, a permanent guest in his brother's house? The attitude of his brother, his niece and nephews, even his sister-in-law's sister—the cripple, Aunt Mattie, in the lodge—leaves him in no doubt. He should give it to them, of course; in their minds, the only question is how it should be divided up. A large slice for repairs to the house, which, with the advent of money, is suddenly discovered to be falling down, an allowance for the nephew to live as a Fellow at Cambridge, extra pocket money for the younger boy, new dresses for all the females, an allowance to Aunt Mattie, and so on. Dudley, a generous individual, is soon left almost poorer than he was in the first place. And at that moment a natural desire—the primary self—asserts itself in him: to have something of his own. He too has discovered a use for his money. He decides to marry, producing consternation in the family, for if Uncle marries, he will want his income for his wife, the allowances will be cut off. . . .

His brother, as head of the household, meets the crisis in a manly way. His own wife having died, he appropriates his brother's fiancée. That pair is now seen walking on the garden path, arm in arm. Dudley yields her up, as though, like his fairy-gold legacy, she could never *really* have belonged to him, and he prepares, when the honeymooners return, to step back into his familiar place in the family—the money will be theirs again since he no longer has a use for it. But another surprise is in store for him. He has been dislodged. His former fiancée has replaced *him* at his brother's side. Edgar no longer has a use for him. At this Dudley rebels; he flees into the winter night, encounters Miss Griffin, Mattie's ill-treated companion, who has been put out of the lodge into the snow. Eventually, wandering about, he falls ill and nearly dies. Nursed back to health by Miss Griffin, he is brought home again. He is reconciled with his brother, who has found, when death threatened to take him, that he could not spare him after all, and the two walk, arm in arm, on the garden path, which, for the family watching at the window, makes a happy ending.

This tale, as can be seen, is proverbial, a series of "graphic" illustrations, like some old framed series of colored prints, with such mottoes as "Out in the Cold," "A Friend in Need," "Reunited." It is strange among Compton-Burnetts for its gusts of old-fashioned sentimentality. Whenever Compton-Burnett writes about sickbeds and nursing, there is an unaccustomed tremor in her voice, but *A Family and a Fortune* has *two* long and very quavery bedside scenes: Blanche Gaveston's illness, which proves to be fatal, and Dudley's. In both cases, as in Victorian novels, there is a "crisis," a sort of medical Rubicon which the patient dramatically crosses to the accompaniment of quickened prose.

"The crisis came, and Dudley sank to the point of death, and just did not pass it. Then as he lived through the endless days, each one doubled by the night, he seemed to return to this first stage, and this time drained and shattered by the contest waged within him. . . . But the days which passed and showed no change, did deeper work. . . ." Similarly, Dudley's flight and meeting with Miss Griffin, to whom he gives his coat, their battle together with the elements, recall climactic episodes in Victorian novels that anticipated silent films, with frenzied program music played by the house organist. All this is well done of its kind, but it is curious to find it in Compton-Burnett, who is noted for her asperity. In fact, this is the most Dickensian of her novels and not only in the bathos. Here, for instance, is the description of Edgar: "He had thick, straight, speckled hair, speckled, hazel eyes, vaguely speckled clothes. . . ." That is pure Dickens, only Dickens would have carried it further until Edgar became one gigantic speckle. Quite a few of the characters in *A Family and a Fortune* (as in several of her earlier books) resemble Dickens' people in being lopsided, like personifications of a single tic or twitch of behavior, though Dickens' mythic extravagance is missing, just as the impulse, here, to sentimental effusion is dryly checked, as if an inner prompter had frowned and shaken her head.

A Family and a Fortune is an unexpected throwback to the Victorian novel. But it is also a sharp revision and correction of it. Take Justine, Edgar's thirty-year-old unmarried "only" daughter, as she always emphasizes, as though she pictured herself cheek to cheek with her parent (who in fact is wholly indifferent to her) in a large group photograph. She is like a Dickens heroine—an older Little Dorrit, the mainstay of her family—but regarded, as it were, through corrective twentieth-century glasses. To the modern reader, a figure like Little Dorritt is unbearably irritating, and that is the case with Justine; the difference is that Compton-Burnett permits her to irritate everyone, and not just the reader. It is as though Compton-Burnett, impatient with the reading matter of her youth, had taken a Victorian author by the scruff of his neck and forced him to *live,* day in, day out, with one of his models of virtue. Not that goodness is unbelievable. It exists, as a cross that others have to bear. Eager, helpful Justine is a trial to her family because she is unfailingly eager and helpful. Her mother, a tall woman, must be for her "Little Mother," and her young brother, of course, is "little boy." Her finger seems to be constantly uplifted, pointing, like a guide showing a recalcitrant group through a picture gallery: "It is a pretty picture, isn't it? Dear Grandpa, with his white hair and fine old face; and Aunt Mattie, handsome in the firelight, vivacious and fluent, and no more querulous than one can forgive in her helpless state; and dear, patient Miss Griffin, thinking of everyone but herself." For her, everything instantly composes itself into a tableau: "Look. Oh, look, indeed! Here is something else before our eyes. What led me to the window at this moment? It is inspiring, uplifting."

Brave, lecturing Justine, always looking on the bright side, always exhorting herself and others, always mediating, is a real heroine, not a false one. What is wrong, then? What is wrong with virtue when it is not a mere mask for vice? For Compton-Burnett, that is a central puzzle, which *A Family and a Fortune* seems to be bent on resolving, at least provisionally and on an empirical basis, and this probably explains the book's Victorian machinery and atmosphere, since virtue, especially in the form of service, was the great theme of Victorian fiction.

In a Dickens novel, Justine would be the Good Angel of her family. Here she is a painful instance of someone who is all second self, whom practice has made horribly perfect, like a child's piano lesson. Her primary self has been firmly eradicated, and instead of being a triumphant illustration of what can be done by will power, she is an embarrassing rebuttal of the case for self-sacrifice, of the "example" she is trying to set everyone around her—her brothers, her mother, her aunt. "Where is that stoic strain which has put you at our head, and kept you there in spite of all indication to the contrary? Where should it be now but at Father's service? Where is your place but at his side?" The suppression of the actual claims of self has made her unremittingly self-assertive and smug in conversation. Similarly, Miss Griffin, another model of self-sacrifice, is shown to be exasperating to live with. Her self-effacement and capacity for service have their natural home in the sickroom—that sickroom which in the Victorian novel so often pre-empts the center of the stage.

Justine's opposite in the novel is her malevolent Aunt Mattie, who, as a cripple, feels entitled to exercise power. Her physical powerlessness is her claim on everyone's attention, just as her lack of money constitutes a lien on Dudley's. She is all primary self. Not in a position to give, she is ungenerous in receiving, which is another way of saying ungrateful. Mattie is a false martyr (she is too egotistic to mind being a cripple), coupled with a real martyr, the unfortunate Miss Griffin. Like Justine, she is a compulsive talker, but Mattie's speeches are intended to be read *between* the lines. Her specialty is insinuation. Her true meaning, usually the reverse of what she says, slowly becomes apparent, like writing in invisible ink when dipped in the appropriate chemical. In short, Mattie is the covert as opposed to the overt, exemplified by the blunt Justine. What is shocking in Mattie, though, is her failure decently to conceal her naked, primary self. When she turns Miss Griffin out into the night, she shows her true colors, but in fact she has never hidden her hatred, envy, and malice; she has only feigned to hide them, as she feigns not to understand the meaning of her own words or, for that matter, the words of anyone else, which she likes to take in their opposite sense, twisting them to her purpose.

The principal verbal contests in the novel are between

Mattie and Justine, closely matched partners, with Justine playing umpire as well, naturally, and seeing "the good side" of her aunt. Her adamant insistence on doing so may even constitute a victory, which suggests that virtue is more crushing than vice. The relation between aunt and niece is complementary, like the relation between Edgar and Dudley—two halves of a whole. There are no "complete human beings" here, only halves or fractions. At bottom, *A Family and a Fortune* discloses a dichotomy in human nature, a "law" which enjoins a separation between one and one's true self as radical as that between the rich relation and the poor relation. Those in whom the true self gets the upper hand, if only briefly, are dangerous; the true self, like the poor relation, must be taught to keep his distance. Yet those who have conquered their worse selves or do not possess one have no real place at all. The moral would seem to be that everyone ought to have something to hide but they ought to hide it successfully, as Blanche Gaveston has done until her deathbed delirium, when abruptly this devoted mother, who has lived only for her children, makes clear her disappointment at life's ungenerosity. "Are you my beautiful daughter? . . . The one I knew I should have? Or the other one?" Justine does not recognize the unspeakable. "I am your Justine, Mother."

February, 1967

The Writing on
the Wall

The Collected Essays, Journalism and Letters of George Orwell is very sparse in letters. The war and the bombing partly explain it. But Orwell was not much of a correspondent, and the people he must have written to, *e.g.,* his parents, evidently did not save his letters. In four thick volumes, only one to his mother turns up, one to his wife, Eileen, one to Sonia Brownell, whom he married in his last illness, none to his father or his sisters. He writes his publisher that the older sister, Marjorie, has died and he will have to go up to Nottingham for her funeral, and footnotes let us in on the fact that the younger one, Avril, was actually living with him as his housekeeper after his wife's death and taking care of his adopted son. Did he never leave a note on the kitchen table when he went out for a walk or write her during his absences to inquire how things were going? Not a word from Burma, where he spent more than five years in the Indian Imperial Police; four letters (one partly business) and a postcard from Spain, during the Civil War. It was mainly publishers, editors, his agent, his executor, writer friends—people with office space and the professional habit of filing documents—who duly kept his correspondence. This gives a bleak impression of a life.

From April 1939 to January 1940, there is a blank; you would never know that the war had broken out on September 3 and that he was trying to enlist in the army—quite a reversal since when last heard from he had been violently opposing a war with Germany, declaring that it would result in the "Fascization" of England and that the British Empire was worse than Hitler. Such epistolary blanks, like holes cut out by the censor, surround the principal events of his life, both in the private sphere (what led to his marriages? did he never write a love letter?) and in the sphere of politics, where so much of his passion as a writer and journalist centered.

Take Hiroshima. It is first mentioned in his regular "London Letter" to *Partisan Review*. You would expect some further reactions in letters to his friends on the Left. Nothing. Ten days after Nagasaki he is writing to Herbert Read about organizing a Freedom Defense Committee, *Animal Farm,* the death of his wife, which had happened some months before, a holiday he plans to take, Labor Party politics, the doings of common friends. Since he has been emphatically approving (May and July 1944, in a polemic with Vera Brittain in *Tribune*) the saturation bombing of German cities, using the argument that "it is probably somewhat better to kill a cross-section of the population than to kill only the young men" ("I . . . object to the hypocrisy of accepting force as an instrument while squealing against this or that individual weapon"), the reader is curious as to how he will "take" the atom bomb. Later (October 1945, "You and the Atom Bomb"), he foresaw the enormous significance of nuclear weapons in maintaining an international balance of terror and a political status quo within the super-states, but what happened in between, what caused him to revise his common-sense, let's-cut-the-cackle defense of the practice of total war, is not revealed in these volumes. There was something in Orwell that made him jib at the atom bomb, maybe what he called "decency," yet whatever it was, quirk or deep moral sanity, remains to be guessed at.

Or take the gas chambers. Though he was in Germany as a reporter shortly after the surrender, he seems to have been unconscious of the death camps, which just then were being discovered farther east. No letters, apparently, have survived from this period, or perhaps he did not write any. The dispatches he sent to *The Observer* and *The Manchester Evening News* have not been reprinted here (presumably for lack of interest), but in his regular journalism he continues to speak of "concentration camps," as if he did not know about the extermination camps or as if unaware of a difference—impossible to tell which. He speaks of Dachau and Buchenwald and asks almost in the same breath, "Is it true about gas ovens in Poland?" We never hear the answer. You will not find "Auschwitz" or "Genocide" in the index, and Orwell's attitude toward atrocity stories is sometimes that of the plain Englishman rendered suspicious of "propaganda"; the departure from the average represented by an atrocity put a tax on his powers of belief. At other times, his interest in atrocities, such as it was, concentrated on the reluctance or eagerness of the public to believe in them. For him it was a wry study in human credulity or incredulity—itself a form of credulity when belief is withheld automatically. He tended to write war crimes off as committed inevitably by both sides and hence, on the balance sheet, canceling each other out. If the crucial fact of Auschwitz finally "got to him"—he lived, after all, until 1950 —the record is amnesiac.

In view of the uncanny "natural selection" which has decreed, as though according to his wish (he wanted no biography done of him), that whatever was intimate or revealing in the private letters of the man who became "George Orwell" should perish, the survival of the first letter in this collection, dated 1920, is all the more extraordinary and dramatic. Of the hundreds of schoolboy "missives" he must have penned in his copperplate handwriting, why should this one—and this one only—have come to light? Eric Blair, aged seventeen, is writing to a school friend from his family's summer home in Cornwall: "My dear Runciman, I have little spare time, & I feel I *must* tell you about my first adventure as an amateur tramp. Like most tramps, I was driven to it. . . ." He goes on to explain how, taking the train from Eton for his summer holidays, he unwisely got out of the carriage at a station, was left behind, missed his last connection, and was stranded for the night in Plymouth with sevenpence ha'penny, where he had a choice of staying at the YMCA for sixpence with no supper or buying twelve buns for the same money and sleeping in a farmer's field. He chose the second and passed a cramped, cold August night surrounded by neighboring dogs that barked alarmingly at his every movement, reminding him that he could be put in the clink for fourteen days—he understood that "frequently" happened if you were caught on somebody else's property with no visible means of support. "I am very proud of this adventure," he ends, "but I would not repeat it."

Such a relatively unadventurous adventure has been granted to many middle-class children: missing your train, being stranded without money, sleeping or trying to sleep in a cold, uncomfortable, *illicit* place in great fear of detection. I once slept in a confessional box while running away from home and, another time, aged fourteen or fifteen, I spent most of a cold night roaming about the back yard of a university student I loved, dressed in my first evening gown (yellow chiffon with a silver belt and a bunch of cherries at the waist) with a bottle of poison in my hand. I too was unnerved by the barking of neighboring dogs and also by the clatter of garbage-can lids, which I must have jostled as I passed, in my new silver slippers, to match the belt; a bride of Death was the principle of my costume. Though eager to die, I was terribly fearful of being caught trespassing before I could swallow the iodine and be discovered on the premises as a corpse.

In that charade, no necessity was operating. I was not "driven" into an action that might have led a suspicious person to call the police. I could equally well have killed myself in my own bed or at the washbasin, leaving a note. Yet in fact the young Eric Blair did not *have* to pass the night in a farmer's field in some "slummy allotment." As a Shaw reader, he must have known about the Salvation Army. Obviously an alert internal prompter notified him that here was his chance: *carpe diem*. Indeed, his letter to Steven Runciman sounds as if the idea of being a tramp was something they had often discussed at school. Now he had done it and was happy to furnish the details.

Ten years pass before Blair is heard from again, and now he is addressing an editor, enclosing an article he has written: "The Spike." It is an account of one of the casual wards where he has been sheltering, with other derelicts, while tramping through the south of England. Soon, rearranged, it will turn up in *Down and Out in Paris and London,* the first published book of "George Orwell," who was contriving to bury Blair in more senses than one. Before assuming the identity of a part-time tramp in England, he had been working as a dishwasher and kitchen porter in Paris. He picked hops in Kent as a migratory laborer (described here in "Hop-Picking") and made an effort to penetrate the inside of prison life by deliberately getting himself arrested as drunk and disorderly ("Clink")—a failure; they let him out after forty-eight hours. From 1927 till 1932, in Paris, London, and southeast England, Blair was purposefully moving in the lower depths of society among the wrecks and the jetsam. He was conducting a sort of survey, the reverse of the traditional Grand Tour, of the geography and institutions of these nether regions: workhouses, flophouses, Salvation Army shelters, cheap lodgings, jail. It is clear that he was not doing this for "copy," nor was he exactly forced to it by shortness of money; his favorite aunt was living in Paris all the time he was down and out there, but, so far as one can tell in the absence of any letters, he does not seem to have touched her for a loan.

It is as though, once he had resigned from the Indian Service, he wished to be acted *upon,* rather than to act, that is, to follow the line of least resistance and see where it led—a quite common impulse in a writer, based on a mystical feeling that the will is evil. Blair-Orwell detested and resented every form of power; in politics, he loved rubbing his opponents' noses in reality, the opposite of the corporate or individual will, just as in language he hated abstraction, the separation of mental concepts from the plurality of the concrete. The line of least resistance, obeying a law of social gravity, led him naturally downward to gauge the depths of powerlessness and indignity, and the knowledge he brought back made it impossible for him ever to eat a meal in a smart restaurant again, in the same way as, later, after going down into the English coal mines, he wrote "I don't think I shall ever feel the same about coal again." Every now and then, in those four or five years of vagrancy, Blair surfaced, working as a tutor to a defective boy, staying with his older sister and her husband, staying with his parents, only to plunge back again into anonymity. Was this "coming up for air" a simple manifestation of the life instinct or some complicated testing of his forces of resiliency? By coming to the top he kept his freedom to sink once more, when the spirit moved him. He refused to drop definitively out of sight by an act of choice.

Certainly he was not averse to abrupt decisions: the resolve to fight in Spain (we do not see the resolve forming; here is another of those blanks—he suddenly writes to his agent that he will be going to Spain in about a week, though up to then—December 15, 1936—the war in Spain has not even been mentioned), the resolve to write the book about the coal mines, living in with the miners' families, the resolve to rent a farmhouse on the remote island of Jura in the Hebrides.

That last resolve must have been a long time dormant. In 1940, he had written: "Thinking always of my island in the

Hebrides." But then no more, till, the European war over, his wife dead, a young child they had adopted in his care, it is suddenly a *fait accompli*. The decision was probably fatal, but for the reader, gifted with foresight, every move, starting with that first juvenile "adventure," has been fatal and fateful —a succession of coffin nails hammered home. It was in the cards: death of pulmonary tuberculosis, aged forty-six, University Hospital, London. Q.E.D. Like a spectator at a play of preternaturally tight construction, the reader is gripped with horror, admiration, anger, pity, revulsion as he races through the early accounts (sometimes printed here for the first time) of Orwell's experiments in crossing the class barrier, experiments conducted ruthlessly on his own frame, in a scientific spirit, for though he was a strong believer in individual difference and came to fear, above all, the thought that people would become interchangeable parts in a totalitarian system, he seems to have felt that as a subject for study himself he was a universal, *i.e.,* a fair sample of his kind, capable of normative reactions under dissection. His end has something macabre in it, like the end of some Victorian pathologist who tested his theories on his own organs, neglecting asepsis. In his last letters, he speaks of his appearance as being "frightening," of being "a death's head," but all along he has been something of a specter at the feast. He was prone to see the handwriting on the wall, for England, for socialism, for personal liberty; indeed, his work is one insistent *reminder,* and his personal life—what we glimpse of it—even when he was fairly affluent seems to have been an illustrated lesson in survival techniques under extreme conditions, as though he expected to be cast adrift in a capsule.

Survival interested him greatly, yet the punishment he gave his own body almost insured its rapid decline. It was a miracle he lasted as long as he did, considering. An undiscovered lesion in his lung contracted in his Dickensian boarding-school ("Such, Such Were the Joys"), a bout with pneumonia in the Hôpital Cochin in Paris ("How the Poor Die"), the throat wound from a sniper's bullet during the Spanish Civil War, the first sanatorium, in Kent, the winter in a warm climate—Marrakech—prescribed by the doctors, another illness, the war, rejection by the army as medically unfit, service in the Home Guard, austerity, poverty, assiduous overwork, the cold winter of 1947, the second attack, the sanatorium in Glasgow, the Crusoe-like severities of the primitive island of Jura, which was often cut off from the mainland, near-drowning in a whirlpool and exposure while waiting for rescue, the third attack . . . When his first wife, Eileen, aged thirty-nine, died while he was abroad just after the German surrender, he ought, one feels, to have taken it as a warning signal to himself: what was the cause of her unexplained "poor health"? He does not seem to have wondered. "When Eileen and I were first married," he had written a few years earlier to his friend Jack Common, ". . . we hardly knew where the next meal was coming from, but we found we could rub along in a remarkable manner with spuds and so forth." More than once he speaks of how women of the working class age early in comparison to middle-class women, and it sounds as though Eileen O'Shaughnessy, a Customs Collector's daughter, had embraced a working-class fate in marrying Eric Blair. "Yes, she was a good old stick," he said after her death to a friend who was expressing sympathy.

The consumption that carried off Orwell used to be considered a disease of the industrial poor. It cannot be an accident that so many of the best writers of our century have been consumptive: D. H. Lawrence, Kafka, Silone, Simone Weil, Camus, but also Thomas Mann and Katherine Mansfield, who do not appear to "belong" to this company of prophets and holy outcasts, although Katherine Mansfield was often desperately poor. Tuberculosis, for artists of this century, is what syphilis was for the nineteenth, a sign, almost, of election. But whereas venereal disease was the mark of commerce with Venus (now fully licensed), a lesion of the lung appears among modern writers as a sort of Franciscan stigmata, a mark of familiarity with privation; after all, poverty today, at least in the West, is a "stigma." Most of those tubercular writers can be imagined as constituting a brotherhood or third order outside ordinary society, a brotherhood of intractables. Simone Weil going to work in a factory and eventually starving herself to death in order to share the diet of the people of occupied France was answering the same "call" as Orwell living among the derelicts and hop-pickers or as Silone militating in the underground, in clandestinity.

A copy of *Nineteen Eighty-Four*, translated into Hungarian and secretly passed about, is said to have been the catalyst of the Hungarian Revolution. *Animal Farm*, a precious text too in Eastern Europe, is a political fable that, like *Gulliver*, will probably endure as a children's classic. But surely Orwell's best work is that of his heroic early period: *Down and Out in Paris and London,* "A Hanging," "Shooting an Elephant," *The Road to Wigan Pier*, and finally *Homage to Catalonia*, which ends his novitiate. These terse writings resemble looseleaf pages from a diary, which has *survived* to tell the tale. Or they are like ghostly polished driftwood, not intended for the coffee-table. There was always something unwelcome in Orwell's revelations: the return of the repressed. This note was struck again, hard and fierce, in two later essays, written when he was already famous and successful: "How the Poor Die" and "Such, Such Were the Joys." He would not forget having touched bottom, which assured him of having his feet on the ground.

His book reviews and literary essays ("Inside the Whale," "Dickens, Dali and Others") are not especially acute, except in flashes. His penetration was less literary than moral; he was on the lookout for the hidden flaw in an author. More important historically are "Boys' Weeklies," "The Art of Donald McGill," "Raffles and Miss Blandish." The criticism of popular culture was a genre he virtually invented; it is hard to remember that, before him, it scarcely existed, though there were anticipations of it in the early Rebecca West and in Q. D. Leavis (*Fiction and the Reading Public*). "I have often thought," he wrote to Geoffrey Gorer in 1936, "it would be very interesting to study the conventions etc of *books* from an anthropological point of view. . . . It would be interesting & I believe valuable to work out the underlying beliefs & general imaginative background of a writer like Edgar Wallace. But of course that's the kind of thing nobody will ever print." This gloomy forecast was characteristic; he would not have liked to know that he would be starting a fashion for that "kind of thing."

He was on to something new in "Boys' Weeklies" (1939), but not exactly new to him. He had done something like it, though he may not have noticed the parallel, in his masterpiece, *Down and Out in Paris and London. I.e.,* he was making another *descent*. An exploratory plunge into the limbo of sub-literature, sub-art: cheap stories for boys, comic postcards, thrillers. He was also very much interested in a category which Chesterton had named "good bad books"; he was an avid collector of pamphlets and he had a great memory for hymns and music-hall songs. He enjoyed this type of material and believed that everyone else did, if they would only confess the truth, and, as happens with sports and hobbies, his enjoyment was solemnized by expertise, the rites of comparing, collating, a half-deliberate parody of scholarship like the recitation of batting averages (cf. Senator E. McCarthy).

If there was anything he despised, it was fashion; whatever was "in" affected him with a violent claustrophobia. He wanted out. His first escape attempt was to Burma. On the surface this looks natural enough. He was born in Bengal; his father was in the Indian Service, and his mother was the daughter of a tea-merchant in Burma. Yet if he was following family tradition (he had "worshiped" Kipling as a boy), he was also eluding the career open to his talents; the next step after Eton would have been Cambridge or Oxford, then the London literary world. Instead, he became a policeman. Whatever his parents thought, from the point of view of his contemporaries at Eton he could have sunk no lower. Empire was out of fashion. But from his own point of view the colonial society he found in Burma must have been preferable to the London literary cliques, if only because the second looked down on and snickered at the first.

He hated intellectuals, pansies, and "rich swine," as he called millionaires, and nothing made him angrier during the war than the fact that repairs were being made to the empty grand houses in the West End. He was also incensed at the suggestion that rationing should end. His extreme egalitarianism involved cutting down to size any superior pretensions. He was quick to catch the smell of luxury, material or intellectual; he sneered at Joyce for trying to be "above the battle" while living in Zurich on a British pension, at Gandhi for playing "with his spinning-wheel in the mansion of some cotton millionaire." The luxury of being a pacifist ("fascifist") in wartime drove him into furies of invective; at different times he compared Gandhi to Frank Buchman, Pétain, Salazar, Hitler, and Rasputin. He was capable of making friends with individual plain-living pacifists and anarchists, *e.g.,* George Woodcock, having attacked them in print, but he continued to regard anarchism as at best an affectation (at worst it was "a form of power-worship"); the pretense that you could do without government was mental self-indulgence. What he really had against intellectuals, pansies, and rich swine was that they are all fashion-carriers—a true accusation. Fashion is an incarnation of wasteful luxury (nobody *needs* a mini-skirt), and one thing he liked about the poor was that they could not afford to be modish—a somewhat tautological point.

He did not mythicize the poor (he loathed myths too); he

saw them rather dourly as they were. Their imperviousness to
middle-class ideas was both an argument in their favor and a
reason for despair since they showed no signs of inventing a
socialism of their own, and he did passionately want socialism for everyone, on moral and rational grounds; as he
pointed out, the machine had changed everything: "So long
as methods of production were primitive, the great mass of
the people were necessarily tied down to dreary, exhausting
manual labor: and a few people had to be set free from such
labor, otherwise civilization could not maintain itself, let
alone make any progress. But since the arrival of the machine
the whole pattern has altered. The justification for class dis-
tinctions, if there is a justification, is no longer the same, because there is no mechanical reason why the average human
being should continue to be a drudge." Yet the poor and the
working class, slow to change their habits (and maybe because of this), possessed at any rate "common decency"—a
quality Orwell found absent in many intellectuals and well-to-
do people. "One has the right," he says despondently, speaking of Pound, "to expect ordinary decency even of a poet."
The "even" sums up his feelings. Having no vanity himself,
though plenty of angry pride, he disallowed the claim of the
artist to be exceptional in any way, and here he was flying in
the face of reality. The artist *is* an exception and given a little
leeway, as a matter of common sense. But Orwell did not
have much "give." It is surprising, for instance, to find
him indulgent to Sir Osbert Sitwell. His egalitarian strictness
made him an incipient philistine mistrustful of the vagaries of
art, not to mention the vagaries of the artist.

Indeed, he *was* a philistine, of a peculiar kind, that loved
beauty, flowers, birds, Nature; this curmudgeon even loved
poetry, not just good bad poetry, but the real thing. But it was
a love crossed by misunderstandings, like the love, in some
fable, of one species for another, a mastiff for a rose. He
wrote bad poetry himself and sometimes in his early book

reviews a schoolboy purpled prose. His genius was for precise observation of data and for quantifying, which made him a better analyst of the art of Frank Richards, author of boys' stories, than of the art of Tolstoy. It is easier to quantify "the underlying beliefs & general imaginative background" of a Frank Richards than to apply rule-of-thumb measurements to Tolstoy or Swift or Dickens.

Though aware of the impossibility of it, he would have liked to find some acid test to subject works of art to which would tell the scientific investigator whether they were good or bad. Survival, he typically decided, was the only measure of greatness, but of course this leaves the problem of what causes an author to last. He devised a test for characters in fiction: a character in a novel "passes" if you can hold an imaginary conversation with him. In his own novels, only Big Brother, probably, would meet that eccentric requirement. He was a Sherlock Holmes fan and a lover of puzzles and brain-twisters, also of the odd fact of the "Believe It or Not" variety. His book reviews often turn on the methodical solution of a puzzle ("What's wrong with this picture?"), as when he discovers—quite astutely—that the fault of Koestler is "hedonism," something that is not apparent to the untrained eye. He was not a natural novelist, having no interest in character or in the process of rising or sinking in ordinary society or in a field of work—a process that engaged the sympathies not just of Proust or Balzac but of Stendhal, Flaubert, Tolstoy, Jane Austen, George Eliot, Conrad, Zola, Dickens, Dreiser. He would have been indifferent both to success and to failure. It is hard to imagine the long family-chronicle novel in several volumes he was planning to write just as the war was breaking out. Maybe he did not have enough human weaknesses to be a real novelist.

He was interested in institutions, in whatever could be measured, counted, surveyed, in the mechanics of work, in cost. He inventories his books to find how much reading has cost him over the past fifteen years and gets a figure of twenty-five pounds a year. Calculated out at nine and ninepence a week, this equals eighty-three cigarettes (Players). Most of his books, he notes, he bought secondhand. He was always totting up. He maintained careful records of the minute profits of the small village shop he kept (about one pound a week), of crops planted in his garden, of the milk produced by his goats and eggs laid by his hens. When the war comes, he reckons that he can grow half a ton of potatoes in one year, which ought to see them through the all-but-certain food shortage. And shortly after Munich, he tries to enlist Herbert Read in a scheme to buy printing presses to be ready to get out clandestine leaflets when England goes fascist; estimated cost probably three or four hundred pounds. He is sure fascism is coming because he has added up the possibilities and he "cannot believe that the time when you can buy a printing press with no questions asked will last forever."

In his political speculations he thought in terms of futures and sought out "laws" to ease the labor of prediction (wars break out in the autumn, after the harvest has been got in; the decline of the British Empire was attributable to the invention of the telegraph, which killed off individual initiative and centered decisions in Whitehall), just as when arriving at a spike he sought to find its characteristic defect—every spike had one. He was fascinated by the inner workings of institutions and would have liked to take them apart, like a watch. His inventiveness was of an old-fashioned, hard-headed, utilitarian kind. He had odd hobbies, one-man parlor games. At one time he "tried to devise an envelope which couldn't be opened without the fact becoming apparent." During the war, in his diary, he drew up an Atrocities Table in parallel columns, with dates: those believed in by the Right; those believed in by the Left. After a tabulation and breakdown of famous crimes, he amused himself constructing a model of the popular idea of the perfect murder. Tinkering with the notion of a perfect tyranny must have led him to the construction of the "model" societies of *Nineteen Eighty-Four* and *Animal Farm*. Building these ingenious, Erector-set worlds based on a few simple principles such as double-think and "but some are more equal than others" must have appealed to his sardonic imagination.

He was an unsociable bird and so far as one can tell he held little communion with himself, except to the extent that he was a source of data, the nearest one at hand. He used himself, as I said, as an experimental animal in the course of his social researches. Or as a "control." Hence he had to keep himself under strict observation, and this is especially evident in his early period, when he was a "pure" recording instrument and his writing was most delicate and exact. His celebrated honesty was a workmanly quality. It is a question of keeping your tools clean. A precision tool must be "true," straight as a die.

Later he formed the habit of making avowals to his readers, often in a truculent manner. For instance he admits suddenly that he has never been able to dislike Hitler. Such a confession "expects" that the reader feels the same but has not had the bravado to declare it. The part of himself that Orwell exposes to his readers—and the only part that interests him—is the common man, the man on the street, You and I, insofar as we are capable of honesty. Nigel Dennis said that Orwell's appeal was "to what everyone knows in his heart," but this is less a soft appeal than a challenge, sometimes a species of blackmail or bullying: if you think you dislike Hitler, you are a hypocrite or a toady of fashion and you had better think again. The same with such phrases as "the pansy Left," "the successive literary cliques which have infested this country," "hordes of shrieking poseurs," Blimpish summons to the boor in the reader's heart to emerge with a safe-conduct. "To write in plain vigorous language one has to think fearlessly," he declared. It is true that he did not care what people thought of him, but this may not always be such a virtue as he imagined; the opinion of others is a corrective.

Possibly Blair-Orwell was corrected too often in youth to brook it afterward. Though he tots up for the record the mistakes in prophecy he has made in his "London Letter" to *Partisan Review,* he is generally convinced of his own rightness. Once he has changed his mind he seems to be unconscious of having done so and can write to Victor Gollancz early in 1940, "The intellectuals who are at present pointing out that democracy & fascism are the same thing depress me horribly," evidently forgetting that he had been saying that himself a year earlier: "If one collaborates with a capitalist-imperialist government in a struggle 'against fascism,' i.e., against a rival imperialism, one is simply letting fascism in by the back door." On the occasions when, conscious of a possible previous injustice, he starts out to write a reappraisal, as in the cases of Gandhi and Tolstoy, he slowly swings around to his original position, restated in less intemperate language. In "Why I Write," he declared "I am not able, and I do not want, completely to abandon the world-view that I acquired in childhood." This is loyal and admirable in the man, but it is a grave limitation on thinking. Lacking religion and mistrustful of philosophy, he stayed stubbornly true to himself and to his instincts, for which he could find no other word than "decency." The refusal to define this concept (is it innate or handed down and if not innate what is the source of its binding power?) makes Orwell an uncertain guide to action, especially in the realm of politics, unless he is taken as a saint, that is, a transmitter of revelation—a class of person he had a great distaste for.

It is impossible, at least for me, to guess how he would have stood on many leading questions of our day. Surely he would have opposed the trial and execution of Eichmann, but where would he be on the war in Vietnam? I wish I could be certain that he would not be with Kingsley Amis and Bernard

Levin (who with John Osborne seem to be his main progeny), partly because of his belligerent anti-Communism, which there is no use trying to discount, and partly because it is modish to oppose the war in Vietnam: we are the current, squealing "pinks." I can hear him angrily arguing that to oppose the Americans in Vietnam, whatever their shortcomings, is to be "objectively" pro-totalitarian. On the other hand, there was that decency. And what about CND? He took exception to the atom bomb, but as a "realist" he accepted the likelihood of an atomic confrontation in a few years' time and computed the chances of survival: "If the show does start and is as bad as one fears," he wrote from Jura to a friend, "it would be fairly easy to be self-supporting on these islands provided one wasn't looted." I cannot see him in an Aldermaston march, along with long-haired cranks and vegetarians, or listening to a Bob Dylan or Joan Baez record or engaging in any of the current forms of protest. The word "protest" would make him sick. And yet he could hardly have supported Harold Wilson's government. As for the student revolt, he might well have been out of sympathy for a dozen reasons, but would he have sympathized with the administrators? If he had lived, he might have been happiest on a desert island, and it was a blessing for him probably that he died.

If he is entitled to be called "the conscience of his generation," this is mainly because of his identification with the poor. He was not unique in tearing the mask off Stalinism, and his relentless pursuit of Stalinists in his own milieu occasionally seems to be a mere product of personal dislike. The rigors of his life, his unswerving rectitude entitled him to assume the duties of a purifying scavenger. Nobody could say that Orwell had been corrupted or would ever be corrupted by money, honors, women, pleasure; this gave him his authority, which sometimes, in my opinion, he abused. His political failure—despite everything, it *was* a failure if he left no fertile ideas behind him to germinate—was one of thought. While denouncing power-worship in just about everybody and discovering totalitarian tendencies in Tolstoy, Swift (the Houyhnhnms have a totalitarian society), and in gentle local anarchists and pacifists, he was in fact contemptuous of weakness—ineffectuality—in political minorities. Apparently he did not consider how socialism, if it was to be as radical and thorough-going as he wished, could secure a general accord or whether, failing such an accord, it should achieve power by force.

Actually during the war he was in favor of arbitrary measures, such as the seizure and requisitioning of empty mansions for housing the bombed-out poor—a sound enough notion but unlikely to be accepted by the Churchill government, as he of course knew. Would he have organized and led a committee of the homeless to storm and occupy those mansions? If not, why rail? It is a question whether Orwell's socialism, savagely felt as it was, was not an unexamined idea off the top of his head: sheer rant.

In reality, though given to wild statements, he was conservative by temperament, as opposed as a retired colonel or a working-man to extremes of conduct, dress, or thought. He clung to the middle-class values which like himself in his early period had sunk to the bottom of society. His main attacks were launched against innovations, including totalitarianism, a "new" wrinkle in the history of oppression, and this may explain his revulsion from the atom bomb. "Man," he wrote, "only stays human by preserving large patches of simplicity in his life," a good dictum but hard to carry out unless some helpful Air Force general will bomb us back to the Stone Age. The longing to go back to some simpler form of life, to be rid of modern so-called conveniences, is typical of a whole generation of middle-class radicals (myself included) whose loudest spokesman was Orwell. As a non-crank socialist he was obliged to believe in progress, which involved him in a good deal of double-think; in fact he hated the technology which he counted on to liberate the majority and loved working the land which in any rational socialist economy would be farmed by tractors. When the war finally came, he found an unsuspected patriot in himself, discovering him literally in a dream. He had completed a circle: his first published writing, printed in a local paper (and not reprinted here), was a patriotic poem: "Awake, Young Men of England." The date was October 2, 1914.

January, 1969

Hanging by a Thread

IF you can imagine an auditory pantomime, you will be in the peculiar world of Nathalie Sarraute. A pantomime in reverse, where instead of tiptoeing action and gesture, you have vocables, so to speak, with their fingers to their mouths. In pantomime, the spectator "understands" a dialogue or soliloquy from the signs made by the performer ("He is afraid," "He is arguing," "His feelings are hurt"); in the mime of Nathalie Sarraute, an invisible action or plot—that is, a relation—is understood from snatches of overheard speech, the word in some way reverting to its primitive function of sign or indicator. And just as an "Ouch!" or a "Pow!" in a silent movie has a greater sonority than any "Ouch!" or "Pow!" recorded on the sound track of a talkie, so the action in Nathalie Sarraute emerges from the murk that conceals it with a degree of visibility that is almost immodest.

The action is simplified, conventional, classic—a Punch-and-Judy show, Keystone comedy, or Pearl White cliffhanger—having to do with the seesawing of power in a human group, which can be as large as a mob or as small as a single integer. Some creature is being chased; he makes a narrow escape; they are after him again; he tries to hide, flattens himself against a wall, melts into a crowd, puts on a disguise; they catch him, tear off his false whiskers; he begs for mercy, uttering pathetic squeals. It is always the One and the Many, even and most emphatically when the delicate power balance trembles and oscillates within a palpitating individual heart. In the outer world, alliances and ententes, protective networks, more or less durable, can be made, but within the individual heart there is a continuous division and multiplication. What counts statistically as one person is a turmoil of constant side-changing, treachery, surrender, appeasement; in that sanctum nobody can be safe even long enough to get his breath.

At the outset, Mme. Sarraute's reader, finding himself in this strange and unquiet territory, may be somewhat bewildered. He hears voices talking but cannot assign them to bodies with names, hair-color, eye-color, identifying marks. It is like listening to a conversation—or a quarrel—on the other side of the thin partition of a hotel room; you long to rush down and consult the register. But there is no register in this hotel; no telltale shoes are put out at night in the corridor, and the occupants of the room next to you keep changing just as you think you have them placed.

At the opening of *The Golden Fruits,* a couple were reviewing an evening out: "You're terrible. You could make an effort just once. I was so embarrassed." Husband and wife, obviously. You knew it was the wife talking because in French the endings of adjectives and past participles make the sex of the speaker clear. More important than their difference of gender, which only indicated that they belonged to the great majority of couples (nothing "queer" about them), was the evidence that here was a pair who kept up with the latest cultural currents—currents which would soon turn into a veritable maelstrom engulfing the newly launched novel "everybody" was talking about.

At the opening of *Between Life and Death,* we are again in a literary milieu, but now it is not the novel but the novelist we find. In person. The voice we hear is male, of course—we can gather that right away—and it is describing its methods of work. " 'I always write on the typewriter. Never in longhand.' " At once the reader is aware of a familiar smell—the incense of fame. That man is not just talking to himself. He is on an imaginary stage of some sort, a confident projection of his own ego into the world. Obligingly and doubtless not for the first time, he "acts out" the process of creation. It is a demonstration, like glass-blowing. There he is at his desk, frowning, pursing his lips, shaking his head, screwing up his eyes (to get perspective); he tears the sheet of paper out of the machine, crumples it into a ball, throws it on the floor ("No, it won't do"), puts in a fresh sheet of paper, starts over. Over and over. As often as ten times in a sitting. It goes on like this day after day: "I reread. I tear out the page. I crumple it. I toss it aside." Suiting the gesture to the word, his arm rises and falls, folds and unfolds, like the "arm" of a machine, illustrating the mechanics of production. And his wife adds her voice. Yes, that's the way he works. His study is a mass of waste paper. He throws the rejects on the floor. Some days he comes out reeling. He doesn't hear you when you speak to him.

No doubt remains. He *has* to be a successful writer. If he were a failure, nobody would be interested to hear how he worked, whether he wrote by hand or on the typewriter, how much he revised, what he did with his first drafts, and so on. And the wife's two bits' worth clinches it. When you live with a great man, a perfectionist, you are inured to his precious litter, his bouts of inattention. Her dulled voice implies a public, not just the immediate listeners who constitute a silence around him, but what is known as an audience. The form, then, taking shape in the first chapter, is the interview. Not a single interview, with a sympathetic critic or TV host, such as you would find described in a realistic novel, but dozens, hundreds, *all* interviews boiled down to their purest essence.

Such interrogatories are the modern index to fame, above all in Europe, where the publication of a book is the signal alerting a mass of professional questioners with pencils and notebooks, tape recorders, microphones, cameras. A factory whistle has blown in the communications industry. Amateur questioners too, rising from behind a palm in a hotel lobby, approaching after a lecture, concealed in trains, behind the white coat of the family doctor, the starched uniform of the nurse: "Where do you find your ideas?" "How did you get your start?" "So you make your corrections with a ball-point? You have a 'thing' about fountain pens? How interesting." If it is true that every citizen today believes he has one book in him (the story of his life), then the legion of interviewers, eager for the recipe, the trade secret, is potentially equal to the whole of humanity. The situation in its automatism and inherent repetitiousness is comical, and the author who takes it seriously, swells with its importance, is a fool, like this poor clown onstage talking about the final "mystery" of creation.

Yet already in the opening chapter there is a fly in the ointment. A small voice detaches itself from the reverential silence. It belongs to a woman, and that woman is a writer herself. A budding writer, apparently, because she is so timid. But she too knows what it is to suffer and doubt, tear sheets of paper off the typewriter, crumple them into balls, start over, to lie awake at night. *Of course* there can be no comparison; *she* is not famous; nobody could want to know, except in mockery, about *her* habits of work. Frightened by her own daring, she shrinks back into the circle of the others. A second budding writer, an "I" this time, is pushed forward, struggling; denying any literary ambitions, he flees to safety in the crowd, refusing to listen to the encouragements of the famous man, who remains in the center alone.

In Mme. Sarraute's work, you often find a circle surrounding a single figure, an "it" in the middle, as in a children's game. To be chosen "it," however, is not as enviable as it looks at first. Isolated, you can become the butt of tormentors before you know what has happened; the rules of the game have been changed without a word of warning. You have been betrayed by the "ring" around you who have led you on, maneuvered you into the spotlight by flattery and now start closing in, abetted by your own need of praise and reassurance, the inner traitor, always seeking to join them. This encirclement befell the eponymous hero of *The Golden Fruits,* but we were not privy to the novel's sufferings as it was bounced about like a pinball in the game of taste-making, unable to escape or come to rest on a fixed point, its own selfhood or identity. It was mute, like the medallioned oak door of *The Planetarium,* which could not disclose whether it was beautiful or ugly or so-so. But in the present novel, although we start as onlookers, amused or repelled by a comic spectacle, we are eventually precipitated into the tragic arena of a consciousness, where the "it" stands alone.

The famous man of the first pages, not unaware of his danger, believes he can beat the game by splitting into two, one part remaining in the center bathed in a soft light while his other part, the common man, denying any special talent (it's just a dreary industriousness, he claims; application of the seat of the pants to the seat of the chair), seeks to find a place in the dark of the auditorium. That simple half of himself would like to know, just as much as they, what it was that made him a writer, set him apart. Well, he says modestly, resuming the interrupted "interview," maybe some of it was hereditary. In the genes. He had a Breton grandfather who was a tombstone-cutter in his youth—quite a character; you could almost call him creative, the way he improved on people's epitaphs with inventions of his own. On the other side, he had Italian blood; that grandfather was a shepherd. And as a child he himself had a passion for words. Yes, it went that far back; as long as he could remember, he was playing by himself with words.

Then (a new chapter is starting) the reader is aware of a sort of air turbulence: a disconcerting shift has taken place.

Of time, place, persons? He cannot yet make out. The voices
are using some of the same words and expressions but they
no longer sound the same. Now it is a "she" who is large and
famous, and "he" has become youthful, humble, small. He
has sent her his manuscript, and she has replied with a letter
—such an astounding, generous letter. Reading him, she has
discovered that they speak the same language; it is she, not
he, who should be grateful—for the pleasure he has given
her. A fellow-spirit! At last someone he can talk to without
the usual precautions. He can tell her *anything*. As a child,
she too must have played with words. He is sure of it. Just
like him, in his little crib, with the bars on the sides, pronouncing words to himself at night. They were his first toys.
And when he was a little older, there was one word in particular. . . . Too late he recognizes the trap; her pale eyes are
mocking him. She is not a fellow-spirit but one of the others,
disguised, sent out to disarm him.

Here the novel begins to unfold its complexities. Who exactly *are* the others? Instead of the audience the deluded creature thought was out there, it is a ferocious jury of writers
that is confronting him and disqualifying his claim to "belong." An inner circle has replaced the outer circle, and now,
rudely manhandled, his words echoed with jeers, he finds
himself on the perimeter, unable to gain admittance except on
strict and contemptuous probation. Yet these persons who
are hustling him into a uniform, thrusting him into the lowest
class of aspirants, are not simply writers more securely established than himself. They seem to have some connection with
the public, whose judicial arm they are. Or the public is *their*
judicial arm. Maybe they are critics—an unnatural hybrid of
writer and reader.

It is not only the others drawn into a circle who have un-
dergone this alarming metamorphosis. He himself is changed
to the point where you would barely recognize him. If he did
not hark back to the old business about his childhood and

what pre-determined his "election" to write, he could pass for a simple unpretentious being. It is they who have twisted his words, to use against him. He has only answered the questions they asked him as honestly as he could. He does tear out and crumple and start over. It was true about his Breton grandfather and his unhappy childhood and the game he played with *"héros, héraut, hérault, erre haut."* Truth is no defense. By their fruits you shall know them. Most people have had an unhappy childhood, an erratic ancestor. Who does he think he is?

That naturally is the central question, which the book's central figure is the last to be able to answer. If he says he is nobody, it is a lie. False modesty. If he says he is "somebody," they will laugh at him. No one, when the searchlight has picked him out, can wriggle out of that dilemma or rise above it. The egregious clown of the first chapter loses his outlines, multiplies, subdivides, becomes all writers, bad, good, and indifferent. His fatuity is seen to be merely an aspect of fame. Insofar as we are famous, we are fools, and fame is something we cannot exactly help but which is done to us with or without our eager co-operation. The fame which makes a writer stand out in high relief from the crowd *exposes* him; hence his protests about being no different from anybody else, untalented, a drudge. These protests are usually sincere, though never believed, and if a writer has the folly to complain of his fame, he is smiled at, like a rich person talking about the "curse" of having money. The writer wanted it, did he not? He worked for it. Probably what he really wanted was glory, which, unlike fame, is not a market commodity.

Still it seems to be a fact that the writer is like everybody else—only more anxious, more preoccupied with himself and with the state of health of that alien part of him which is his talent, the part that has the least to do with *him*, and that is, alas, the most in view. Yet something of the sort is true for everyone. The important part of ourselves that constitutes our definition, our outline, cannot be seen from the inside, even if it can be *felt* occasionally in what we think of as our best moments, when we are "in form." The experiencing subject is unsure of his identity, which is objectified for him by others, though in a fragmentary and unreliable way. I cannot trust the mirror for instance to tell me whether I am beautiful or ugly; nor can I altogether trust the compliments—or the reverse—of friends and family, which send me running back to the mirror for confirmation. This ceaseless back-and-forth, commonest among people known as "sensitive" but universal at least in youth, is epitomized in the ordeal of the writer, whose existence, as writer, must be repeatedly confirmed by a public, so that, to quote Mme. Sarraute's title, he is always hanging between life and death.

That it is a life-and-death struggle is evident from the metaphors used in literary journalism. "I murdered it," says a reviewer complacently of the latest novel. "Lethal," say his admiring friends. "Slaughter. A massacre." "Vitriolic." An author, reading over a passage he has finished, sighs to himself: "Dead. Dead. Dead." That in fact is the sole criterion an author employs to judge his own work, as though he was holding a mirror up to the mouth of an unconscious patient. "Fine result," comments the alter ego of Mme. Sarraute's writer-hero. "It's dead. Not a breath of life." "How do you mean, no life?" cries the anguished hero, who imagines he has given his best, all his treasures, to this text. "Why?" "Oh, you know me," the other replies. "I'm quite simple. Very primitive . . . between ourselves two words suffice. As coarse as these two: it's dead. It's alive. And it's dead. Nothing comes through."

For the writer it is not a mere question of success or failure. He hangs by a thread over nothingness, annihilation. He has put, as they say, so much of himself into his book. And there is no one he can rely on entirely, not the public, his publisher, his literary sponsors, not even his alter ego, that faithful companion who is called into consultation whenever a chapter or a passage is "ready to show." He cannot be totally sure of the objectivity of the *fidus Achates*. Maybe there is not enough distance between them. The other may be partial to him on account of their old relationship. Or he may be infected by his masochism, his sickly doubts, and be oversevere with him. Maybe there is too much distance. What if the other is too conscious of the reviewers out there, lying in wait? The interior critic has to keep a foot in that camp as well; otherwise he would be of no use to him. But wholly trust him or not, this friend, second self, arbiter, is all he has in the world, and he clings to him, damp and trembling, readying himself for the verdict. It is what he feared, "knew all along" was coming. A death sentence. Can there be no reprieve? At first the other is final—no hope. Junk it. But at length he is persuaded to take a second look. Together they assess the damage. Right here is where it goes wrong; back there, yes, possibly, there is a part that can be saved. Reanimated, resurrected by these crumbs of comfort, the writer thinks he has the strength to start over. But first he sends the other out of the room. He has to be alone. The other knows him too well. He cannot have him always bending over his shoulder, trying to be helpful.

Before he was able to divide himself into two and establish this "working relationship," his judge was out there, unfathomable, unpredictable, promoting him and demoting him according to some grading system which he himself can never get the hang of. We return, like a team of journalists, to those who knew him when. His mother, his teachers, his schoolmates spotted him from way back as one of "those." They recognized the signs: brooding in corners, taking an undue interest in words, having bizarre aversions to some of the most harmless ones, talking to himself, "awkwardness, shyness, the feeling of being different, superiority." Back then, though they forget it, these were black marks against him in the Book of Life, pointing to a misfit. How can he say such a thing? Now that he is a literary discovery, what he ignorantly thought were black marks turn out to have been gold stars, and claims to have been his original discoverer are inserted in the record. His mother "knew" from birth, when they brought him in to her: "your high forehead, your look of concentration." His teacher has never forgotten his school composition —"My First Sorrow"—on the death of his little dog, run over by a train. An amazing sense of language for a child.

When his first book is taken, the editor employed to "handle" him is familiar with the signs: arrogance, false humility, childishness, unwillingness to rewrite. They are all alike, authors; he knows them like the inside of his pocket. The more in fact the neophyte-hero inches forward in achieving recognition, the more he is treated as a specimen of an already familiar category of persons, as though there were nothing special about him except his having entered that category, whose laws are now found to govern his slightest movement, even his movements of rebellion, whether he is conscious of it or not.

Readers are sure they know where he got this or that detail in his book. These are Mme. Jacquet's fingers. "Don't worry. Nobody's going to tell her." It's no use trying to fool them. They have heard those disclaimers before. There is nothing in the book whose sources they cannot sniff out: "Your entire childhood. I saw it . . . camouflaged, of course." And his secret motivations for writing, all plain as a pikestaff: "a defense reaction," "an unconscious need for revenge."

If he serves tea to visitors, an ordinary tea-kettle turns in the telling and retelling into a samovar, the tea turns into a rare sophisticated blend, and his nervous gestures are "slow, almost solemn," like a priest lifting a chalice. "You seemed to be officiating," reports his mother. His father is confident that he has his number too. When the hero bursts happily in to tell him that his book has been accepted, the father, barely looking up from something he is writing: "How much did they take to publish that?"

Being neither "somebody" nor nobody, like a defective syllogism, the debutant novelist is reduced to an absurdity. His struggles against claims to know him, pin a label on him, file him, are the purest comedy. What is involved is possession, property, the little tickets that are stuck on his work: "Symbolism. Surrealism. Impressionism . . . Comic. Tragic. Ontological. Drama. Psychodrama." One of the funniest passages, a little masterpiece written by an angel on the head of a pin (found in Chapter 12), has to do with a false claim check. An elder pontifical critic has discovered what he calls the main axis of the book, "the point around which the whole work is organized . . . That scene is the empty railway station . . . It's a pause. A destroyed center." But there is no scene in a railway station. The efforts of the hero to retrieve the horrible situation caused by this blunder (which of course nullifies in a flash the critic's very valuable endorsement) amount to a sort of negotiated surrender. They compromise on a room full of empty benches, in fact a ministry. In an early short story there was a railway station. . . .

Yet the hero, though outnumbered, is still a force to reckon with. The others fear him as a spy concealed among them, pretending to be minding his own business while covertly taking notes. Nor is their surmise mistaken, even if they are usually barking up the wrong tree, as with Mme. Jacquet's fingers, which really belonged to a friend of his grandmother's. Knowledge, they think, is power, and in their view, this note-taking is a power play: he has got them where he wants them, in a book, appropriated them for his own purposes. And the criminal may actually be paid royalties for the stolen property he vends. That is why his attempts to hide must be foiled. He must be brought out into the open, expelled from the circle into the middle. A woman pounces: "You know he too is one." That is also why he must be enrolled in the regiment of his fellow-writers, who can keep a watch on him if he tries to desert.

All this belongs to the social comedy of the literary life, recognizable to anybody who has ever taken part in it. The humiliations and vicissitudes of the hero are not very important in the final analysis, except as furnishing merriment. They are just occupational hazards the little fellows have to put up with—at least in outward appearance the great are not subject to them.

But *Between Life and Death* has another dimension, beyond the social, always the cruel playground of comedy: the games people play. In Chapter 8, a book finally begins to write itself, and at once we are on another scale, an immense staircase, as the hero, conquering his fear, ascends from life toward death, and as usual in death he is alone. He is going into the temple, like the child Virgin Mary, climbing the steep steps in Titian's famous *Presentation,* leaving behind the street crowd and the old woman selling eggs on the bottom stair. For the duration of this chapter, we have left the circle; we no longer hear the desperate pitter-patter of running feet, the thud of ignominious falls on banana peels. Instead, we are in a realm of music. It is a ballet of words, which, as force gathers, turns into a march, a triumphal march, with brass winds blowing in the orchestra. Then, suddenly, at the height of exultation, there is silence. Total. The tragic hero is dividing into two, to face his alter ego.

Nothing of the sort—a rending of the veil—has been attempted before, and one would have said in advance that it was impossible, short of demonstration, to show how an author composes, that is, to create with words a sort of program music imitating the action of other words as they assemble on a page. It is all very well for a piano to imitate raindrops or paint to imitate foliage, but how can a medium imitate itself? Mme. Sarraute has done it; she does it twice in the novel—again and even more tremendously in the desperate final chapter, where the writer, older, is uncertain of his music, which often sounds to him now like a player piano with him pumping the pedals but which nevertheless swells out with a greater resonance and more complex harmony until it breaks off.

Of course he is writing *Between Life and Death*. "Take this one to start with, this tiny fragment . . . that arm like the arm of a jointed puppet, which stretches out, folds, drops, that fist that opens. . . ."

This device, of the novel enclosed within the novel (the Quaker Oats box), might have seemed a mere form, not new either, of literary Op art, if the force of it here at the finale did not close on us like Nemesis. We had half felt it coming, we were "prepared," yet we were not sure. So there is only one author, as we suspected, one book, which they all were writing: *this* book, fabricated in solitude, imperfect, conscious of its blemishes, modest, gigantically boastful, daring to enter the arena, expose itself, and contest its right to survival. Just as the encircled hero stands or falls, finally, by his work, his salient into the world and his redoubt, his last point of retreat, so his creator elects to stand *by* him, taking him by the hand, ready to fall *with* him, naked both, saying "We."

The infinite regress of the Quaker Oats box expresses also the "mystery" of creation, for the nearer you draw to that process, the less you understand it. "Mystery" in ironic quotation marks, yet it *is* a mystery, despite the fact that ignorant people are content to call it that, knowledgeably—as though in pronouncing the word they had somehow taken possession of the thing itself and were jumping all over it shouting its name— "It's a mystery, that's all there is to it. We're in the presence of a mystery." The force of repetition kills eternal truths; that conviction obsessed Flaubert, whose *taedium vitae* took the form of a horror of banality. In this literally double-faced novel, facing inward and outward, like the year god, mischievous, sly, glinting occasionally with malice, but also somber, tragic, heart-shaking in its directness, Mme. Sarraute has undertaken something very bold—the rescue of banality from itself.

Every bromide uttered by her hero and his sycophants proves to be true—specious but true. Whether you feel it as truth or imposture depends a good deal on the tone of voice. Is he preening himself on tearing out and crumpling or is he confessing it, confiding it, mentioning it? There is a whole slithery gamut of nuances. "I have to admit I'm a perfectionist"—what is false about that sentence? Working very carefully, with a pair of tweezers, we may be able to detach the inverted commas from that "confession." It is rare that we find a direct lie when they have been removed—*i.e.,* that the speaker is a shiftless loafer. Usually the inverted commas have sprung up there as the result of mirror-rehearsal or repetition.

In the next-to-the-last chapter, the self-important novelist of the first chapter is back again, older and more munificent with his clichés and precepts. With a shudder, the reader recognizes that voice. " 'We should pay attention to no one. To no one. And to nothing. Except to this.' He lays his hand flat on his chest." Of course he is right, insofar as what he recommends is possible. Everyone would agree. But, more than being right, this old whore has somehow become rather sympathetic. He too has a deflating, puncturing double, though you would never have imagined it, to hear him talk. *She* knows that he is finished as a writer, ready for the funeral parlor. He sees her sitting out there in the circle, who all know it too. She may even be his self-effacing consort. They think he has not guessed it himself but they are wrong. How could he not guess when he senses her *here,* in his plump chest, where he has just reverently laid his hand?

Having kept company with a succession of other, shyer novelists, we are no longer deceived by the façade he showed us when we first met him. At present we see how it is for him, inside, and there no differences exist: all are alike.

In fact for Mme. Sarraute's hero banality is the irritant that gives rise to the work of art, whose worst enemy, by the way (as we saw in *The Golden Fruits*), is good taste. The banal, the "common," which offend the connoisseur, excite in the artist a morbid sort of itch that fatally asks to be scratched. A vulgar, drawling pronunciation. Such overheard sentences as "If you keep on like that, your father will like your sister better than you." Tiny parcels of living substance around which words begin to dance their ballet or mobilize like iron filings in the presence of a magnet. With a little guidance from the author, a current is made to run from the living substance (which may first appear as an effluvium oozing from a crack in the wall that separates each of us from others) through the dancing, wheeling words, which come out faster and faster, in a jet. He watches them perform, moves them about slightly, withdraws one very gently, like somebody playing jackstraws, so as not to upset the structure, and substitutes another. By preference they should be ordinary words (farewell *héros, hérault, erre haut*), in working clothes; an unfamiliar word in Mme. Sarraute's own novels is likely to be found in the dictionary marked *"Fam."* (familiar). A local irritation caused by vulgarity produces an excretion, as with the oyster and the pearl, but the stream or spray of words that come from it (the metaphors keep changing) must retain some of the insipidity, flatness, of the original sickly substance.

The name given to the particle of living substance, the germ of the novelist's novel, is simply *la petite chose*. If other people try to assign a more precise name to her ("A vulgar accent, that's all; you mustn't let it get under your skin"), he is furious; they are taking her away from him, but she is his. As the book progresses, this humble creature, a sort of Cinderella, assumes a more and more important role. Now there are three in the novelist's workroom: himself, his double, and *la petite chose*. It is almost a crowd.

By the final chapter, success has altered the relations between them. His double is no longer his plain old friend; he talks in a new stylish way, betraying the time he has been spending in literary circles. "Alive" and "dead" aren't good enough for him any more. He has his nose in a big grammar —the one critics use to trip up an author. Sometimes his voice cannot be heard over the voice of the crowd. The worst, the most alarming sign is that he is no longer as critical as he used to be. Don't worry; just publish it, he says. Everything between them is upside down. Now it is the "I" who is suddenly captious, wants to improve, rewrite, but the "You" brusquely stops him. You're crazy. Leave it alone. How cynical he now is about the public! "They'll never notice the difference" is his attitude. Or doesn't he care any more himself?

Evidently he is lost to the hero, who has no one to turn to in his extremity. All he can hear is the other writers out there, sneering at him for the enormity of his ambition to join some of them on their pedestals. The wider public seems to have disappeared. It is dark. But he is not utterly alone. *La petite chose* has stuck by him, after all, despite the mistakes he has made with her, painting her up, sending her to the great dressmakers. In fact, they have become closer, since the double has been unfaithful. *She* has not changed; she still has that stale, musty smell he has a perverse liking for. Feeling her there, he takes heart again. He dares another look at the chapter. And lo, as though recalled, reassured, by the nearness of *la petite chose*, his double is once more at his side. Not too close, says the author, but not too far off either. They look together at the chapter, examine it for signs of life. It seems to be faintly breathing. Is it the hero's imagination or does his old friend observe too a fine mist on the pocket mirror placed before its mouth?

The book, naturally, ends on a question, the question asked by all books: Am I alive or dead? The answer, if by that is meant the reception, is material for *The Golden Fruits*.

Indeed, the hero of the present work in his most aghast moments could not have foreseen what happened. Did it get bad reviews? Good? Mixed? It got no reviews. It came out in the month of May during the Paris general strike, when there were no newspapers or magazines, no television, and radio that consisted of news bulletins. By the time the media were back in service, the spring publishing season was over. Everyone went away for the summer, and when they came back, it was the fall publishing season. Nobody was talking any more about the books of last spring.

What happened to *Between Life and Death* was a common fate. Democratic. Covered by the act-of-God clause in the contract. Any book published in May was killed instantly, without suffering. A good way to go. Some lingered as a memory, in a few bookstore windows; a few people bought them, probably. A brief notice or so may have followed, in the fall or winter—not reviews but oversights remedied. Perhaps there has been somewhere a real review of *Between Life and Death* that I missed. All that is sad but funny. It belongs to the comedy of the literary life. What is important is that the book was written. It exists, compact in itself, independently of the sum of its readers and having a kind of self-evidence like a theorem in geometry. Soon somebody will find it, in a train or a hotel or even a bookstore: "I never knew she wrote that." Though it is less a "born" classic than *The Golden Fruits,* it is more original, more complex, larger, deeper. Its greatest originality, more striking than its bewitching technical resources but leaning on them for support, is its egalitarian view of its subject. Hence the strange appropriateness of its being killed during the May-June revolutionary events; it would not have minded that. In any case it is an heroic book, as much a deed as an imitation of one, and therefore merits not fame but glory.

July, 1969

One Touch of Nature

THE absence of plot from the modern novel is often commented on, like the absence of characters. But nobody has called attention to the disappearance of another element, as though nobody missed it. We have almost forgotten that descriptions of sunsets, storms, rivers, lakes, mountains, valleys used to be one of the staple ingredients of fiction, not merely a painted backdrop for the action but a component evidently held to be necessary to the art. The nineteenth-century novel was full of "descriptive writing"; a course called that was still given at Vassar when I was an undergraduate. How innocent and young-ladylike that sounds, like the push-pulls and whorls of Palmer Method penmanship.

We have come a long way from the time when the skill of an author was felt to be demonstrated by his descriptive prowess: Dickens' London fogs, Fenimore Cooper's waterfalls, forests, prairie, Emily Brontë's moors, Hardy's heath and milky vales, Melville's Pacific. Yet in their day these were taken as samplings of the author's purest creative ore, his vein of genius —more even than character-portrayal or plot handling. In the old triad of plot, character, and setting, the setting, comprising Nature and her moods, supplied the atmosphere in an almost literal sense; it was the air the novel breathed, like the life-sustaining air surrounding Mother Earth.

The set-pieces of description in the English and American nineteenth-century novel correspond with the primacy of land-

scape in English painting. *The Mill on the Floss* brings back
Constable and vice versa. In the fresh delicate strokes of
George Eliot, Mrs. Gaskell, Hardy, there are affinities with
the water color and the sketch: Cotman, Turner, the notations of Ruskin, and again Constable, his skies, woodland,
weirs. But the English novel is also redolent of the prepared
oil painting. Hardy's landscapes with cattle, his markets and
fairs suggest the English animal painters. Dickens evokes
coaching scenes, and his lurid sunset Thames recalls Turner.

On the Continent, there were the hunts of Turgenev and
Tolstoy, the forest rides of Madame Bovary, Tolstoy's peasants reaping and threshing, the sawmill in Stendhal. On the
whole, though, there is less easel scenery in Continental fiction
than in our own; a simple test is whether you can skip the
"boring parts"—*i.e.,* the descriptive passages—without missing some of the action. It is easier to do this with Melville or
Hardy than with Flaubert, where Nature is more functional,
as in the famous contrapuntal scene of the Agricultural Fair.
And with an author like Adalbert Stifter (*Colored Stones*),
the test works in reverse: if you skip the snowstorm in "Rock
Crystal" or the Hungarian plain in "Barbara," you will have
no story left, for these tales are deposits of Nature, like mineral
specimens on which a few spores of human life have survived.

Yet allowing for differences in the treatment of landscape
and the elements among the "old" authors, most of them had
in common a notion of Nature as belonging to the cast of
characters of a novel—sometimes as a chorus, jeering or sympathetic, sometimes as one of the principal actors, even the
prime antagonist, the role it inevitably plays in stories of the
sea. The obvious exception is Jane Austen. There Nature appears as a shower interrupting a walk, a source of wet feet,
drafts, and colds, and this matches the scarcity of physical description of her characters. You know how much money her
people have but not the color of their eyes. Another exception
is Dostoievsky. Yet in Jane Austen's moral scheme, Nature

or, rather, the natural—the reverse of affectation—is in fact a guarantor of value, just as it is in Shakespeare, whereas in Dostoievsky, the unnatural (an unnatural crime, unnatural sons, unnatural desires and impulses) has become the most natural thing in the world, and no evident reason can be found in the nature of things—though perhaps one exists, finally—to argue against a student's killing an old pawnbroker. For the modern town-dwellers of Dostoievsky (and this is *where* he is modern) there is nothing "outside." Even virgin America, in *The Possessed,* instead of being an Eden, is a scene of gang labor and sordid exploitation, not an unspoiled wilderness but a pestilential cabin.

Among the writers of our own century, it is chiefly Faulkner who sees Nature as a force in human destiny, and he also shares with the nineteenth-century Naturalists an interest in genetics and the inheritance of traits; the word "nature," after all, derives from *nascere:* birth, natality. It is your "born" hand. Joyce too, though in an urban setting, insists on what is "outside"—river, sea, strand, elm ("tell me tale of stem or stone"), the snow in "The Dead" falling softly over Ireland, a universal blanket or shroud. In *Finnegans Wake* the snoring Earwicker is the hero of a cosmic Nature myth, where the thunderstorms popular in nineteenth-century fiction become the actual onomatopoeic growl of thunder in the most primitive Indo-European language. Joyce, however, is not interested in genetics (which have a "plot," mutation, a "story-line") but in the static Family of Man: death and resurrection, sleeping and waking. At the same time, his famous seesay (*Ulysses*) is also a seesaw; what is "outside," for Stephen Dedalus, has lost its absoluteness and sovereignty and is only a flickering series of notations on the perceptual screen. This fall into relativity is even more emphatic in Virginia Woolf. It is felt in Proust too, though with a difference, since he learned from George Eliot and Ruskin, for both of whom Nature was a moral law. But for Proust what is outside is inconstant, depending on the "way" you elect to take, like the peculiar optics of the church steeples near Combray, which appear to move as the viewer's position changes.

Such confusing stunts, including mirages, quicksands, the ventriloquism of the echo, "painted" turtles, the mocking-bird, all the monkey tricks of animal mimicry constitute Nature's freak show and tend to produce the opposite of a sense of sacred awe. This is evident in the case of Nabokov, a professional lepidopterist and amateur of botany and ornithology. There is a great deal of Nature in him but also a great deal of affectation. For him the natural world is the clever artifact of a showman closely resembling the artist-as-prankster; the curio cabinet of his fiction reveals a schoolboy's hoard of specimens, human and non-human, collected and mounted, with a special partiality for the ephemerids, like the nymphet Lolita, impaled on pins. At the other pole, perhaps illustrating a class difference, is the sentient Nature of Lawrence, bred in the coal pits, whose language trembled with wonder on approaching a single wild flower.

For Lawrence, as for Faulkner, something formidable exists beyond man-in-society and beyond the natural sciences as well, something both innate and transcendent. Faulkner's sole inheritor on the contemporary American scene is Mailer, who treats himself on the one hand as a natural force and on the other as a culture-hero, a hell-harrier, Herakles cleaning the Augean stables and putting on the shirt of the Centaur when making out his alimony checks. He can describe a bear-hunt (*Why Are We in Vietnam?*), make symbolic use of a deer park, and introduce a living elephant into his latest non-fiction epic (*Miami and the Siege of Chicago*). His competitor, Bellow, tried something of the sort with *Henderson the Rain-King* and with the eagle in *Augie March,* but Nature is not Bellow's "scene"; when he touches this wild material, it turns into fable, not myth. Henderson in the lions' den is a figure in a Talmudic vaudeville.

On the Continent, this side of the Iron Curtain, the natural world is in almost total eclipse. There was no Nature in Gide, not much in Mann or Malraux; there is none in Sartre, very little in Moravia. With the exception of Silone, among the Continental writers considered important today, the outdoors, at best, has a sort of hallucinatory presence. The blinding sun in *L'Etranger* which causes the hero to commit a murder, the sinister North African mountain in Claude Ollier's *La Mise en Scène,* the frightening lizard on the wall of *La Jalousie* are all in some way abstract or cryptic, signifying the retreat of the outside from cognition. The tropisms of Nathalie Sarraute, which refer to biology, are little darting movements of attraction and repulsion of the life-substance enlarged by the novelist's microscope. For the "new" writers, far from being a touchstone of value, Nature is a source of disquiet, an unknowable quantity; the more minutely an object is studied as it impinges on the perceptual screen, the more mysterious it becomes, owing to the lack of perspective. Nature is not a reference-point, outside man, giving the scale, but inseparable from the viewer and his cognitive processes, themselves thrown into doubt.

Surprisingly at first sight, considering the empty landscape of the recent novel in France and Italy, there is quite a bit of weather, usually hot. But where the weather in the nineteenth-century novel supplied mood music for the characters' reveries, aided or interfered with their projects, as it does in life, here it subjects them to a more or less uniform pressure (Moravia, Duras, Robbe-Grillet, Le Clezio, Ollier); it is "close," confining, an atmosphere productive of aberrations, as in a terrarium. And this is true even when, exceptionally, the oppressive climate is northern as in Butor's *L'Emploi du Temps,* set in the pervasive gray damp of an English industrial town, itself as hallucinatory to the hero as a rainy jungle of the Amazon.

In general, landscape, where found at all in the recent Western novel, tends to be exotic, tropical, or sub-tropical, Mexican, North African, Central African, Greek-islandish, Capricious, and this of course reflects average contemporary experience, for which the outdoors is strictly a vacation area, pictured in travel brochures and airline advertising. Already the safaris and duck-hunts of Hemingway had less in common with the hunts of Turgenev and Tolstoy—or with Lawrence's "The Fox"—than with the present-day escape industry, in which seasonal expatriates and fashion models, following the sun, look for unspoiled corners of the earth to despoil. Even his early fishing-stories, set in the North Woods, struck a mannered and self-conscious note; compare *Huckleberry Finn*. What betrays the bad faith of Hemingway is the invariable intrusion of the social into a natural context: hierarchies, exclusions, competitive brio. He is concerned with behavior, which he confuses with action and conduct. Among his American followers, *anti*-social behavior may be inserted in the outdoors, with incongruous effects; consider the skin-diving hero of James Jones's *Go to the Widow-Maker* (the title is from Kipling) masturbating, in his snorkel, in a deep-sea cave.

But to understand the disappearance of what might be called the normal outdoors—sunsets, birds, trees, fields, pastures, waterfalls—from the contemporary novel, it is important to recall that it was not always an important presence. The great explosion of Nature into fiction occurred in the nineteenth century. Early in the century descriptive writing had abounded not in prose but in the verse of the Romantic poets, though actually, in England, the *plein air* movement of poets and poetry had begun in the Age of Classicism. It coincided with the Industrial Revolution (begun circa 1750), that is, with the erosion of the countryside by the dark satanic mills. Thomson's *The Seasons* is usually given as the demarcation point, following Wordsworth's claim that between *Paradise Lost* and *The Seasons* (about sixty years), English poetry, with two exceptions, does not contain "a single new image of external nature and scarcely presents a familiar one that seems to be drawn directly from experience and worked on by imagination." In fact the Romantic poets may have represented the last spurt of an impulse found in Thomson, Cowper, Collins, Akenside, even Crabbe, not to mention Blake sitting naked with his wife in his garden. Still we see Nature-worship less in Blake's tiger or Collins' weak-eyed bat than in the effusions of their successors. Hymns to Mont Blanc, "Lines left upon a Seat in a Yew-tree . . . on a desolate part of the shore commanding a beautiful Prospect." Wordsworth had the habit of leaving his verses behind him, to be reabsorbed by Nature in her metabolic process, as though his bardic utterance were some sort of organic material: "Written with a Slate Pencil upon a Stone, the largest of a Heap lying near a deserted Quarry." He kept copies, however, which went in the normal way to the printer.

As everyone knows, the Romantic poets were fond of the common wild flower—the celandine, oxlip, field daisy, snowdrop—of autumn leaves, larks, and cuckoos, that is, of Nature in its most ordinary and minute particulars. But the words "desolate," "deserted" point to the true Romantic taste in the outdoors, a taste you do not find in the previous generation of stay-at-homes. For Wordsworth and his circle, the "little unpretending rill," the "Brook whose society the Poet seeks," the field of yellow daffodils, but even more kindling to fancy, lakes, mountains, lonely shores—what used to be known as "scenery."

Scenery, a word seldom used nowadays, could be defined as Nature arranged in purple passages for the traveler. In principle, you have to travel to find scenery, which was the only kind of Nature Byron responded to; Shelley too had a liking for Promethean vantage-points of a sort not found in rural England. But Wordsworth and his friends accepted the ethical task of showing that scenery was also distributed democratically, in small units, in your own back yard; the lesser celandine should produce the same moments of exaltation, of communion with the infinite as a mountain pass or the roaring ocean. This is the burden of Coleridge's beautiful poem "This Lime-Tree Bower my Prison," where he regrets that owing to an injury he cannot accompany his friends to a waterfall and wild dell where the adder's tongue and mountain ash grow but comforts himself for the loss by seeing "good" in the humble-bee and the bean-flower and ivy of his own domestic bower, shaded by lime and walnut. More prosily, Wordsworth actually wrote a poem to the "Spade of a Friend (an Agricultural-ist). Composed while we were labouring together in his Pleas-ure-ground."

There is no doubt that Romanticism, as practiced by this circle, was a social doctrine—a protest against industrialism and the reification of man by technology. In "The Excursion" (1814) Wordsworth declaims against the pollution of the countryside by the manufactories. A bell of doom rings out over the afternoon fields calling children and women as well as men and boys to work the night shift of the cotton mill; yet the poet is under no illusion that rural toil, as he observes it, is much better. He has gone beyond the whistling farm-boy of *The Seasons* running happily behind the plow: "Our life is turned   Out of her course, wherever man is made   An offer-ing, or a sacrifice, a tool   Or implement, a passive thing em-ployed as a brute mean." This is an echo of Kant, and in the poet's criticism of industry, there is a foreshadowing of Tol-stoy: "A bondage lurking under the shape of good—   Arts in themselves beneficent and kind   But all too fondly fol-lowed and too far—." In this poem, he is also worried by the population explosion. The balance of Nature, such as he had known it in his boyhood, is being undone by industry, by the robotization of the farm laborer, and by demographic in-crease. The only remedy he perceives is universal education plus migration to the colonies; he fastened his hopes for Eng-land on the Empire. . . . As for the poet himself, opting out

was the sole resource. The Romantic protest forlornly anticipated the hippie movement by more than a hundred and fifty
years: Coleridge's and De Quincey's opium, the colony of
friends in the Lake Country, where Coleridge, city-bred, re-
joices that his child will grow up by "lakes and sandy shores,
beneath the crags of ancient mountain. . . ."

This savage scenery, which was associated with a sense of
freedom, also revealed itself to the Romantic painters. Nature
painting, as such, came in with the Romantic movement:
peaks, cliffs, caverns, storms at sea. Landscape had entered
painting in the Renaissance, as a background to a portrait or
as the sympathetic setting of a sacred event—a Nativity or
Baptism or Transfiguration. Snow-covered distant peaks, appropriately, were first seen in the Swiss painters of the
Renaissance, *e.g.,* Hans Fries. And before the Romantic
period there was the landscape painting of Poussin, classical
in design but tinged with Romantic feeling; there were
Claude Lorrain, Cuyp, Ruysdael, Gainsborough, Richard
Wilson. . . .

Roughly speaking, the pre-Romantics saw Nature in her ordered aspect, as the classic *rus* of the Eclogues and Georgics,
while the Romantics saw it as wild, insubordinate, elemental.
The classic *rus,* whose goddess was Pomona, was a celebra-
tion of the *routines* of Nature, the calendar of agriculture. It
is the same classic *rus* you find in a great deal of pre-Romantic
verse, above all in Crabbe and in Thomson's *The Seasons*. The
classic *rus* is the harbinger of Romantic Nature, both in poetry
and in painting. It is the barn swallow preceding a great flight
of eagles. Or the hay wain as a Trojan horse out of which
would spring the wild horses of Géricault and Delacroix.

Yet this distinction, which would admit the hunters in
Breughel's snowy scene, has a hard time comprising Claude
Lorrain, on the one hand, and Ruysdael, on the other. Another difference, perhaps more significant, is that in Romantic
painting for the first time (or almost, leaving out the animal
painters) you find landscape with no people in it. No gods or

goddesses, no peasants, no picnickers. Just empty Nature, clouds, trees, waves, rock, waterfalls. Here Ruysdael must be counted as the great precursor; those lonely brown woodlands traversed by mysterious roads, like the arteries of some unknown life-system, appear at first glance utterly uninhabited, and the tiny figures that can usually be descried at second glance were put in by an assistant, to satisfy seventeenth-century convention: Ruysdael, it seems, did not know how to paint the human form. Or did not care to learn. Aside from some tawny vegetable-like cottages, the ribbony roads leading nowhere were the sole allusion he was capable of making to man's presence in the universe. The painter was alone with Nature. This did not occur again for more than a century.

Solitude marks the change, just as in poetry. The Romantic poet, wrapped in a cloak, contemplating the sea, the mountains, the desert, was the unique spectator: Shelley on the Euganean Hills far from the "polluted multitude." And something of the sort seized the novel a little later in the century. The characters were held offstage, while the author communed with Nature, penning a description of the setting and the accompanying weather. A nineteenth-century novel frequently opened with a panorama of the region, which eventually narrowed to pick out a single small figure crossing the poetic space. Think of Cooper's *The Prairie* or the wonderful aerial perspective of the first chapter of Manzoni's *I Promessi Sposi,* with the "camera" swooping down to focus on Don Abbondio. Or Egdon Heath and the reddleman. Or the "questionable" sound of the weaver's loom coming from a stone cottage at the start of *Silas Marner,* not far from a deserted stone-pit.

Generally, in a novel, the convergence on a single figure or group of figures in a bare unpopulated landscape foreshadows a grim outcome, for the novel is a social medium; the poet may be led to inspired musings by an encounter with a leech-gatherer, but such a meeting in the first chapter of a novel would symbolize doom. Nature, whether man-ordered (Horace's Sabine farm) or pure and undefiled, like the Muses' spring, has always figured in literature as the opposite of Society. The town is the moral wilderness, if it is only a village or hamlet, but this moral wilderness is the novel's stamping-ground, and indeed there is a territorial imperative that appears to call country-bred heroes and heroines to the town in order to complete their novelistic destiny: Emma Bovary, Julien Sorel, Tess, Pip, Jude, Renzo in *I Promessi Sposi*.

In parenthesis, it ought to be said that in modern times the old antithesis between country and city, virtue and vice, still holds but with the difference that farmland and pasture and orchard are no longer equated with Nature in her purging, purifying aspect. This is particularly true in America, where "the great outdoors" is by convention limited to the West, the Southwest, the North Woods—ranch country, Hemingway country, rattlesnake country, bear country, ABM country. This notion, which has belligerent moralistic overtones, identifies Nature with bigness. When Senator Joe McCarthy was preparing for his great crusade against "Communists-in-government," he did not retire to the Wisconsin dairyland to replenish his forces by contact with Mother Earth. He went west to Arizona, where he found "real Americans without any synthetic sheen on them." This ranch life, doubtless based on a frozen-food locker, was Joe McCarthy's version of Romantic pastoral.

It is possibly no accident that Romanticism in politics and literature originated, with Rousseau, in Switzerland—the home of "scenery." Rousseau's natural man, alienated by institutions from his true self, is of course a fictive creature, like McCarthy's "real Americans," viewed as the salt of the earth, non-iodized. Yet if the reality of this fiction is accepted, if man-made institutions are regarded as a conspiracy against Nature or against man's natural goodness incorporated in the nation, then obviously the tall timber or the desert is a better school for re-education than the farm. But if, on the contrary, country life with its routines is looked on as a repository of precious traditions, stored like preserves in the buttery, the farm, with its dependencies of woodland, grist-mill, carpentry-shop, and so on, becomes the point of contact between man and animals, man and the seasons, man and the vegetable and aqueous worlds. That is how Tolstoy saw it, opposing what was false to what was natural, in human behavior as well as in medicine, art, law, and farm methods, and the natural, for Tolstoy, included a great deal that had been learned, over centuries, and that it would be unnatural to forget, as people in society are wont to do. Thus civilization is an organic accumulation or compost, to which the common people, that is, the peasantry, have more ready access than the bureaucrat or the worldling, both of whom may appear as boors or primitives in comparison to the God-fearing rustic. The earmarks of the natural are not always apparent to logic (serfdom, an "historical" institution, was an unnatural state of affairs, *i.e.,* evil, whereas the village commune, another long-standing institution, was natural and good), but common sense, more prevalent among simple people than among the educated, was the faculty, almost like an animal instinct, by which the truth could be recognized. The characteristic, in fact, of truth for Tolstoy was its recognizability; the truth (compare Socrates) is what we have "always" known. Hence truth and Nature are the same; both are *there,* at once outside man and in his heart.

This view, which is easily confused with the doctrines of Romantic politics since both oppose Society in its urban forms, does not assume, however, a natural goodness in man or in Nature either; rather the reverse, as can be seen from Tolstoy's picture of war as a blind force unaccountably sweeping the world and moving bodies of armed men back and forth across the map slaying and killing, like the destructive sexual passions, which rise and subside. War is a truth, seemingly permanent, which cannot be explained away by historians seeking proximate causes, which, if not present, would have obviated this or that conflict.

Despite Tolstoy's dislike of Shakespeare, there is much that is Shakespearean in his sense of Nature, including the importance he assigns to the truth-finding faculty of common sense —in Shakespeare usually embodied in women, fools ("naturals") and non-participants. Yet for Tolstoy, passion, however destructive, is always superior to tepid good conduct, and this no doubt is a prejudice of epic and dramatic authors. In Stendhal, passion, the capacity to feel it, is the great and unique virtue: Madame de Renal, the Sanseverina, Count Mosca's jealousy. It is the untainted font or spring that gushes up from elemental sources, like the libertarian energy released by the arrival of Napoleon's army in Milan. In a way this is surprising, for Stendhal is one of the most worldly of novelists, interested in power and the dynamics of social leverage. Julien Sorel, in *Le Rouge et le Noir,* is a bundle of contradictions. The son of a carpenter in the Savoyard region of the River Doubs (his career seems a parody of Our Lord's, down to his martyrdom and burial in a marble-garnished grotto, mourned by two weeping women and a faithful disciple), he is a breath of mountain air in the salons and drawing-rooms of the Restoration. At the same time, this priest-educated child of Nature is handicapped by an inability to feel; he cannot respond appropriately to the "supreme moments" of passion offered him in all genuineness by Madame de Renal. Whether the inability to feel what you are *supposed* to feel is natural or unnatural is hard to decide with Stendhal, who probably did not know himself. Julien's malady is in part attributed to the choking-off of the energies of the Revolution by the "black" hand of reaction; the same point is made in *La Chartreuse de Parme,* where Fabrice, a "natural child," a byblow of the French Revolutionary armies, a spontaneous being who *can* feel, is walled up in the prison of a tower, like a bird in an aviary.

Sudden tonelessness of feeling, a sort of psychic frigidity, is related, in Julien, to social ambition; as a "new man," he is worried about how he should be *behaving,* and Nature in a careerist milieu is not a very reliable prompter. That frigidity and self-watchfulness are found repeatedly in the nineteenth-century novel: in Emma Bovary, Frédéric Moreau, Dickens' Pip, whose great expectations have stunted the lively natural boy brought up in the country "by hand." Tolstoy and George Eliot noticed the phenomenon, which they connected with intellectual and bureaucratic activity (Mr. Casaubon, Count Karenin) and which, peculiarly enough, was accompanied in the sufferer by a sense of immense solitude, as though estrangement from Nature and total immersion in it, as in the case of the Ancient Mariner, could produce the same effect.

Most of the best authors of our own time have advocated, in one way or another, a return to Nature or a radical simplification of society; D. H. Lawrence, Orwell, Mailer, Solzhenitsyn might all be classed as cranks or drop-outs. Faulkner, when in the city, insisted on styling himself a "farmer." At the same time the worst political movements have at least one plank in their platforms advocating the restoration of something natural, whether it is the right to carry weapons ("Register Communists, not guns") or the right to untampered-with drinking water ("Stop fluoridization"). The back-to-Nature impulse —natural foods, natural farming, freedom from state interference—is probably felt in equal measure by long-haired hippies in a desert community and members of the John Birch Society. Moreover, the logic of this impulse is generally anti-social and defiant of the majority. A return to Nature implies not merely a rejection of the mechanics of modern life but an actual conviction of being poisoned by their effluvia, whether identified as smog or the mass media or doctored H_2O from a state reservoir. A desire to burrow in the ground, below the contamination level, is seen in the vocabulary of radical youth,

with their so-called underground press, and in the stockpiled
shelters of the Minute Men.

When we are conscious of a loss of Nature in our lives, we
are conscious, most of all, of a loss of solitude. If we complain
about the defacement of the countryside and the rash of ugly
houses that have broken out like a skin disease on the face of
Nature everywhere, we are not only appalled by the wholesale destruction of scenery but by the sense of invasion this
gives us—where can a man hide himself? The Romantic poet
brooding over a maelstrom, the Solitary Reaper, "She dwelt
among the untrodden ways"—such images already (the contrary of *Robinson Crusoe*) identify the human footprint with
pollution.

A man in Nature, truly so, is a man alone, plowing a fur-
row, climbing a mast, tracking an animal. Or if the man is not
alone literally but participating in a group action, such as
reaping or hauling in a fish net, he can still be "at one" with
Nature, because the rhythm of the bodies makes them work as
as a single body—a human implement. An *awareness* of being
"at one" with Nature, however, itself begins to constitute an
intrusion. That is, two fishermen pulling in a net on the sea-
shore appear natural, but two poets brooding side by side on
the same strand would be ridiculous—one solitude too many.

At this point a definition is called for. What are the criteria
by which we can recognize Nature? First of all, everyone
would agree that a pool in a forest was Nature while a goldfish
bowl was not. Second, if Tolstoy was right (and I believe he
was), Nature is antithetical to Society but not to civilization.
The works of man—agriculture—are so woven into the primal
fabric as to be a second nature. This is plain even to the most
insensitive tourist in an "old" country like Tuscany where
windbreaks and olives and grapevines seem inseparable from
the geological pattern of peaks and valleys making up the
original scenery. The land has been husbanded or married

by man. Its mountains have been quarried and mined; its rivers fished and dammed.

Take it visually. A weir in a river appears as a natural fact, and so does a watermill or a windmill or a haystack. To the painter's eye the windmills are a feature of the landscape of Holland, just as though they had grown there. And a thatched peasant's cottage seems as much a part of Nature as a bird's nest; indeed, it is a sort of bird's nest. The painter's eye does not distinguish between a house designed by a bird for itself and a house designed by a cottager for himself. They are both products of Nature.

The reason is that a peasant's thatched cottage, like a bird's nest, was not designed by an individual but by the species. And the form and materials of the dwelling at once identify the species of the occupant, just as with birds: the conical whitewashed *trulli* of Apulia, the bamboo and straw huts of Indochina, the chinked log-cabins of the North. . . . This is only another way of saying that the design is traditional and that local resources—brick, wood, tufa, reeds—have been taken advantage of; in the mountains behind Carrara marble is used for sills. And it is why a palace, like Versailles, despite the aging process, can never be a part of Nature, while a peasant's house can, even if it is not very old. Versailles was a rhetorical vehicle for self-expression of a series of kings. People often wonder why modern houses should stand out as eyesores in the country though not in the city. This is because in modern design every house is conceived palatially, *i.e.*, as a manifesto of the personality of the owner or the ideas of the architect who drew the plans for it. It makes no difference whether these "palaces" are the result of cheap production or not; they are no longer the nests of the poor.

In the same way, for the painter a castle can be an intrinsic part of Nature, for real castles are simply border forts, designed by a species for protection from its enemies. Like the web of a spider or a flycatcher plant. A castle can be solitary, silhouetted against the sky, while a palace can only be lonely, and often is mythically—the palace of the Beast in "Beauty and the Beast" or a tycoon's palace on Fifth Avenue. A cottage on the Polish plain can be solitary, behind its dense paling of lilacs and raspberry bushes, while a ranch house can only be lonely, even if its next-door neighbor is only fifty feet away or whatever the zoning law allows. The horror of modern ranch houses or of modern colonial cottages is the stench of loneliness they give off.

The question of ruins is interesting. It is probable that if Versailles were to go to rack and ruin, be invaded by nettles and wild flowers, it could be viewed as a natural spectacle, less moving than a ruined abbey or temple, more perhaps like a shipwreck. The taste for ruins, a Romantic symptom, became epidemic in nineteenth-century verse and fiction ("Tintern Abbey," "Ozymandias," the eerie scene at Stonehenge at the end of *Jude the Obscure,* the Roman amphitheatre in *The Mayor of Casterbridge,* Daisy Miller in the Colosseum); the wreck of great undertakings symbolized the vanity of human wishes and the final word spoken by Nature. To evoke such sentiments, the dimensions of the ruin seem to be important. A derelict hut is merely unsightly and testifies less to the awesome powers of Nature than to the neglect or misery of the owner. It is customary to muse on the amount of labor invested (the Pyramids) by anonymous, insect-like men. Abandoned quarries, of which there must have been a great number, and mine-shafts overgrown with grass play a melancholy part in English nineteenth-century fiction and verse: Stephen Blackpool, Dickens' pariah weaver, meets his end by falling into the Old Hell Shaft in the country near Cokestown; the deserted stone-pits filled with water by the house of that other pariah weaver, Silas Marner, yield up a robber's skeleton and Silas' money-bags, and at those same stone-pits, in wintertime, a woman has frozen to death.

Abandoned, deserted, overgrown—the test of Nature's presence is some vivid indication of man's defeat, a test not met, say, by a junkyard or by beer cans floating on the sea. Nature is present if a man can feel himself solitary in the spot he is, alone in the world which is nevertheless alive with his fellow-creatures, birds and animals, fish and fowl. What we receive from Nature and the consolation she is supposed to offer us is the sense of being in the presence of something greater than ourselves—larger, more perduring, grander. The immemorial oaks. And though immense vistas, mountain peaks, and the "peaks" of achievement represented by the grandiose columns of defunct edifices can lift or depress the spirits by measuring the diminutiveness of man, smallness in the sentient world, the world of live things, is suggestive of time everlasting, eternal return. The immemorial bees or the dragon-fly, not the immemorial hog.

Nature is not just the circumambient ensemble of non-human life but history on a grand scale—duration. She gives us the awareness of being an instant reverberant in time, clear and distinct as the echoing sound of our footfall in a silent forest or the plash of a stone dropped into a pool. The repetitive cycle of Nature is a promise of eternity. And man in Nature is aware of his singularity in the midst of species; this is solitude. Other men do not disturb him, so long as they blend with Nature in some work-nexus of species-activity; for instance, a row of anglers on a riverbank, each lost in contemplation, the parallel rods making what appears to be a natural and immemorial Sunday pattern.

Yet this sense of being a part of a great Whole (". . . the winds and rowling waves, the sun's unwearied course, The elements and seasons . . . all declare For what th'eternal maker has ordained The pow'rs of man. . . ." Akenside, "Nature's Influence on Man," 1774) has its dark side, especially when pantheism is substituted for the design of the Maker. The permanence of species is made up of individual deaths. Hence the biological cycle, as witnessed by human consciousness, is full of menace, and Nature is seen as the unmoved spectator of human grief. Tennyson, at the age of fifteen, on hearing that Byron was no more, rushed out into the woods and carved on a rock the words "Byron is dead," as though the wounds inflicted on the senseless stone could make the Whole cry out with him.

Nineteenth-century literature is extremely ambivalent on the subject of this two-faced spouse embraced instead of religion. On the one hand, rapture, the desire to be an Aeolian harp played on by the winds of the infinite; on the other, fear. Wordsworth's wonderful account, in *The Prelude,* of the sensation he had as a boy in a purloined rowboat of being chased by a lowering mountain peak (". . . behind that craggy Steep . . . a huge Cliff, As if with voluntary power instinct Uprear'd its head . . . With measur'd motion, like a living thing, Strode after me."), the indescribable threats emanating from Egdon Heath, from the moors, mine-pitted too, of *Wuthering Heights,* from the accursed coal country, masked with wheat and beetroot, of *Germinal,* from the red-lit autumnal Thames River, a fishing-ground for cadavers, of *Our Mutual Friend,* from the moonlit Adda, so still and serene, that Renzo crosses in a boat in *I Promessi Sposi.* Not to mention the treacherous sea and the numerous thunderstorms and downpours, like the one in *L'Assommoir* that attacks the wedding-party huddling beneath a bridge on the Seine.

Nature is not friendly to the lonely hero; it is out to "get" him, singling him out, it often appears, with mere idle destructiveness, as a lightning-bolt chooses to strike a particular tree. And it is true that these nineteenth-century heroes have no lightning-rods; they are orphans in the storm. The quality of being unprotected—by education, family, good sense, worldly experience—is particularly evident in the heroes and heroines of Manzoni, Emily Brontë, Conrad, Hardy, Zola, that is, in those authors where Nature, all but personified, is a predominant force. The more the characters are isolated in Nature, the bleaker their lot. Nor is it just a question of poverty. Compare the penniless Fanny in the populous "social" milieu of *Mansfield Park* with the helpless Tess. Or Dickens' Esther Summerson with the human scarecrow Jude. Or within a single novel, Lucia in *I Promessi,* who has the the protection of institutions, however dubious, with the lone Renzo at the mercy of the elements. In Society, virtue, like truth, compels recognition; outside this context, virtue is not even a quality; in Nature, there are only strength and frailty. From a novelistic point of view, there seems to be safety in numbers, and of course this applies to the human species, by which I mean that it is only for men in numbers, the race itself, that Nature can promise survival, or at least that has been so up to now.

Curiously enough, landscape painting here shows a development similar to that of the novel. Once the crowds of human figures were subtracted from it—reapers, skaters, shepherds, cottagers, huntsmen, and dogs—the landscape became melancholy and almost saturnine, the more so if such man-made natural facts as watermills, bridges, haystacks, wagons, huts were subtracted too. Without these punctuation marks, aids to composition and indicators of scale, the painter, alone with Nature, confronted an incomprehensible abstraction. This has worked both ways: contemporary non-figurative painting, when it does not base itself on geometry, tends to be "read" as landscape.

Any work of literature in which Nature is deployed as a force—*War and Peace, I Promessi Sposi, The Mill on the Floss, Moby Dick,* the novels of Hardy, Conrad, Zola, *The Wild Palms, Doctor Zhivago*—is strangely twofold, at once a dark epic and an idyl. They are cosmic myths, sometimes quite frightening ones. And like cosmic myths, they tend to have a standard plot. Forces are loose in the world—war, drink, disease, monomania, sexual passion—which behave like floods or tornadoes. The "senseless" apparition of Napoleon in Russia is very like the apparition of the Imperial army in *I Promessi Sposi*. *"Passano i cavalli Wallenstein, passano i fanti di Merode, passano i cavalli di Anhalt . . . passa Furstenburg. . . ."* They enter the peaceful Milanese, with its cottages housing spinners plying their useful trade; they ravage it and they leave it. Without rhyme or reason. With them comes the plague, which rages and then subsides. The plague is a symbol of them, and they of the plague. Nobody can foresee when the impetus of either will spend itself, as with one of Hardy's "twisters": "The President of the Immortals . . . had finished his sport with Tess." Those dreadful visitants from the Germanic lands are viewed by the country people as a periodic natural scourge, and yet the havoc they wreak, the crimes they commit are felt to be "against Nature," though their depredations are as natural to their time-honored profession as buboes are to the Black Death. The industrious spinners of the region are simply another and weaker species, like the solitary weavers of English fiction— poor crazed Silas Marner at his toil is likened to a spider. The indigenous great and strong, personified in the *Innominato* (the Nameless One), are another traditional natural element preying on the humble. When this operatic *daimon* finally desists, having seen the light—Lucia—it is as though an insensate whirlwind had been calmed and redirected by a spirit.

The *Innominato* has something in common with Captain Ahab, who has pitted his destructive will not just against the White Whale but against the ship's community, for which whaling is work or labor—the point of man's normal interaction with Nature and in which each "hand" has its assigned part. Ahab's sin, like that of the Ancient Mariner, is an economic crime: the wilful part endangering the whole by a deed of *personal* violence against one of God's creatures.

In the novels of Zola, economics is itself a superhuman force. A human being or family or social group is slowly consumed by agriculture, coal-mining, the theatre, alcohol (the workman's demon), by the sex market, by art (*L'Oeuvre*), by speculation (*La Curée*), or simply by a mania for shopping (*Au Bonheur des Dames*). Many of these subjects seem remote from natural scenes of the sort found in earlier authors, yet Zola is the only Naturalist to have a real conception of Nature. What happens to his characters is a sort of rich decomposition, which not only illustrates the modern waste of human resources but also their fertility. In his vision, even a department store has organic life, like that of a voraciously feeding plant, stealing the nourishment and light of its small neighbors of the ribbon and drygoods business. All the institutions described by Zola are heavy feeders—an idea also found in Dickens, though with less precise knowledge of their habits.

Hunger and its perversion, greed (*La Ventre de Paris*), together with work, the means of satisfying their demands, are Zola's great themes. He is at his best with poor working people. His passion for documentation allowed him to descend without impiety to the underworld of labor, where his lyricism discovered the sources of primal energy—not Virtue, but Nature with her sleeves rolled up. One of the most lyrical passages of nineteenth-century fiction is the scene in *L'Assommoir* of the quarrel in the laundry, where half-naked washerwomen, like strong goddesses, pink and damp, fight with each other in a mist of steam and a Cytherean foam of soapsuds. In the same book, Gervaise's wedding lunch is an epic of eating, a banquet of spiteful and inebriate gods and satyrs, which ends with somebody's throwing the apple of discord. In *Germinal,* the mine-shaft where pit-ponies labor condemned for life to eternal darkness is certainly the bottom of hell but it is also Vulcan's forge. Zola's half-medical interest in genealogy is Homeric; he was writing a modern theogony containing, as happened with the Olympians, many misalliances. The idea of an interrelated primal novelistic stock, the children of Kronos, reappears in Faulkner and is suggested in Tess's connection with the ancient Durbervilles. At the same time, Zola's mythic force is connected with his pictorial faculty; his scenes compose into pictures, which often recall the Impressionist painters—the boulevards of Pissarro—as well as Degas' gas-lit world. As happened with those painters and somewhat differently with Cézanne, whose friend he was (it used to be thought that *L'Oeuvre* was based on Cézanne's "failure"), his sense of light and weather irradiates the most ordinary and humble material. Naturalism without Nature is simply depressing.

The effects of the Industrial Revolution on innocent natural life were apparent to writers, as I have indicated, almost from the beginning. What was not so noticeable was that, owing to the population shift to the cities, farms and isolated cottages were reverting to Nature in the other sense—burdock, brambles, sheer vegetation. The classic *rus* came under double attack. This trend, which has continued right up to the present time, makes nonsense of our old sense of a benign and ordered harmony in which the human species is inserted. It is not only a question of polluting the little unpretending rill but of the encroachment of a new sort of wilderness on the human construct. In the actual countryside, as opposed to the suburbs, there are probably more untrodden ways than there were in Wordsworth's time—abandoned logging trails, overgrown paths, derelict farms, orchards, and pastures.

Well-meaning efforts to save the scenery from real-estate developers and oil refineries, to create wild-life preserves and national park areas (strictly regulated and policed by rangers) do not and cannot re-establish Nature in her natural place. Modern moves to conserve a patrimony of mountains, gorges, rocky promontories, unspoiled beaches, are like moves to save stage scenery—prop trees and painted flats. It was a Romantic heresy to worship Nature in its elemental majesty, far from the vulgar herd, and to identify the poet with the soaring skylark, on the one hand or shrinking celandine on the other. To the extent that Nature has to be defended from man (with the inevitable recourse to police power), instead of being intrinsic to his species-existence, it is simply a backdrop, a photogenic setting, and has nothing to say, one way or another, in determining values or revealing truth. Indeed, the notion, still harbored by every reactionary heart, including my own, that Nature is itself a value, has become subject to opinion, like any other matter of taste, as is shown by the fact that nobody will give his life to defend Yosemite or the Appalachian Trail. At most a small contribution, a bequest, or a letter to the newspapers. This proves that Nature is no longer the human home.

It cannot be a coincidence that modern physics, by interfering with Nature, has for the first time posed a threat to the species and perhaps to most other forms of organic life on earth. And here is another "coincidence": the scientific development leading to nuclear fission and then rapidly to fusion is presented as—and maybe really was—a logical process beyond the power of the human will to arrest, in short as possessing resistless qualities assigned to natural phenomena such as hurricanes. In fact it appears that hurricanes today can be "salted" and epidemic disease brought under control whereas technical advance is a force "outside" man and "bigger" than the brains that conceive it. Technology, originally associated with the civilizing arts of building and weaving, has replaced Nature as the Number One opponent of human society. And technology too has its two faces, its "good" and its bad—good in quotation marks because the benignant side of modern technology, unlike that of sunlight or rain, is not yet demonstrable.

The untoward, uncanny appearance of such a pseudo-natural force on the human scene was noted by Zola and by Hardy—the two nineteenth-century authors who joined an interest in the work-process with a dramatic sense of Mother

Earth. Take the description in *Tess* (which would be omitted in a modern "shortened version") of the new mechanical reaper: two broad arms of painted wood forming a revolving Maltese cross and appearing in the field at sunrise like a second Phoebus with a "look of having been dipped in liquid fire." Or in the same novel the description of the new itinerant steam-thresher and the engine-man with a heap of coals by his side: "a dark motionless being, a sooty embodiment of tallness . . . a creature from Tophet . . . in the agricultural world but not of it. He served fire and smoke; these denizens of the fields served vegetation, weather, frost, and sun." The ousting of traditional tools by machinery ("the engine which was to act as the *primum mobile* of this little world") coincide with the depopulation and dehumanization of landscape, and the author wrapped in contemplation of solitary Nature—the encroaching heath—was in fact saying a last farewell to the pantheistic illusions that fevered Wordsworth's brain in the Simplon Pass, where rocks, crags, raving streams, clouds, and so on "were all like workings of one mind, the features Of the same face, blossoms upon one tree Characters of the great Apocalypse, The types and symbols of Eternity. . . ." As for the poetic effusion itself, far from being an utterance of the Universal Soul, it was coming to be seen as the product of a rather widespread sub-species of humanity that secreted within itself a gland like that in the spider functionally adapted to the spinning of webs.

September, 1969